MISSION
UNSTOPPABLE

Tony —

Stay the course bro',

(301) 520-4348

MISSION UNSTOPPABLE

EXTRAORDINARY STORIES OF FAILURE'S BLESSINGS

PRESENTED BY

GEORGE FRASER
AND
LES BROWN

Presented by: George Fraser and Les Brown

Producer: Ruby Yeh

Editorial Director: AJ Harper

Print Management: Book Lab

Cover Design: Otis Spears

Book Design & Typesetting: Chinook Design, Inc.

ISBN-13: 978-0-9891792-6-3

Printed in the United States of America

CONTENTS

CONTENTS

CONTENTS

GEORGE C. FRASER

INTRODUCTION:
THE DAY I CHOKED AND NEARLY FAINTED

Heart pounding so hard I was sure people could hear it, beads of sweat welling up on my brow, I stood before one hundred people waiting to hear me speak, and I was… speechless.

Three years into my career at Procter & Gamble I was elevated to management responsibility. I had a key role in our new brand release, and I was called on to make a large-group presentation to senior supermarket buyers and executives.

The night before, my boss had come in so we could review and rehearse, but I didn't see the need. I hadn't told Procter & Gamble that, while I was excellent at one-on-one presentations, I had never stood at a podium to make a speech or even made remarks to a large group of people. Still, I was cocksure and ready. Because I had succeeded as a salesperson, I believed I was all that and a bag of chips. I thought, "Why tell them? How difficult could this really be? I got this."

Man, was I wrong. When it was my turn, my memory went blank. I froze. One hundred people sat in stunned silence as my mind filled with dread and my knees began to buckle. I literally could not speak. I felt as though I was about to pass out, to faint right there in front of my colleagues and superiors and our clients and buyers.

My boss, who knew me well and saw the signs, walked briskly but elegantly up to me, grabbed me by the shoulders and said, "George, you must be suffering from the effects of that flu bug we discussed last night."

I felt like a limp wet rag as he escorted me from the room and sat me down. He helped me calm down and catch my breath.

As the world stopped spinning and my heart rate slowed to normal, my mind was full of negative chatter. "I'm good one-on-one, but I'm not a speaker," I told myself. "I never want to do this again."

Defeated, sitting outside the room where I expected to shine and dazzle, I was ready to give up on ever speaking before a group again, no matter how small. But, it was only a string of moments,

I believed I was all that and a bag of chips.

held together by embarrassment, by my need to hide and lick my wounds. My negative talk was a response to a gross failure, but it was only temporary. I knew I would get up, mind the lessons I learned and get back on the horse. I knew this because that's who I am; it's who I have always been.

My sister Emma says I have the ability to "walk through land mines as if they were omelets." In the face of trauma, when others expressed rage or anxiety, I remained silent. I stayed focused and kept moving.

Growing up, I was a "smart ass jerk" with the attention span of a fly. Why? I grew up on the mean streets of Brooklyn, New York, living in toxic foster homes in the projects of Bed-Stuy. I was always hungry, frightened and poorly clothed. My siblings and I suffered gross abuse of every form imaginable. The last thing I was interested in was school; I was interested in finding a way to make money, so I could eat, dress properly and survive my circumstances.

To that end, I shoveled snow, cut grass, raked leaves, delivered newspapers, had a lemonade stand—extra sweet lemonade so customers would buy a second overpriced cup. I started a domestic service to help old ladies clean their homes (then raided their refrigerators) and I started a male babysitting service to watch young boys so their parents could go out and play. My sales pitch was so good I had more business than I could handle, so I hired my brother Joseph and sister Emma to work for me for a sixty-forty split (I got the sixty).

In school, I only liked two subjects: English and history, so I excelled at reading, writing and speaking. Graduating with a "C" average, I wasn't considered "college material." Still, these interests and my trajectory followed me throughout life and got me almost any job or business I wanted.

After a short, successful career selling Encyclopedia Britannica and then starting my own business selling Black history encyclopedias and almanacs in the fiery sixties—great timing for my brand "Black Educational Development"—my good friend Norman Thomas, CEO of RAN Associates, asked me to interview for the "mother of all companies": Procter

I was always hungry, frightened and poorly clothed.

& Gamble. Norman was hired to find "qualified" African Americans to enter the ranks of the illustrious "P&G," the creators of "branding" and the beast of global marketing. Usually, to get in the door of P&G, you needed a Harvard MBA cum laude. I did not feel either credentialed or qualified to get the job, so I did the interview as a favor to Norman.

Nine interviews later, I was hired. With no degree and no experience, I was thrown into the lion's den of "white corporate privilege." I was not alone, but I felt alone. Although I was scared and curious, I was confident I could survive for a few years. I had at least two big things going for me: my entrepreneurial track record that required excellent selling skills and this package that God put me in. Yes, I was light, bright and almost white with "good hair"

3

and standard English diction. I was a very safe choice, although that was never stated or implied.

The velvet handcuffs of a good, stable and prestigious corporate job did wonders for my new family, self-esteem and skills building. After my failure in our group presentation, I knew that even though I could find a way around my fear of public speaking and ascend the corporate ranks, I was not wired to do that. My grand failure forced me to seek the answer to the question that would determine my life's purpose. Something told me to try again; I had the obedience to listen and the discipline to do the work, go through the pain and stay the course. That is how I'm wired.

So I asked myself, "What did you learn?" And after I discovered the answers, I declared: "You've got to do better."

You could read every single book on swimming known to man, become an expert on the literature and instruction of swimming, but until you jump in the water, your ass can't swim. You have to actually do it. I knew I would have to get up and speak and, over the course of the next year, I found ways to do it. I made it

**My failure was a blessing that
led me to my mission.**

my business to find opportunities in my community to stand up and talk to people about something I felt passionate about. Every speech, however short, no matter how small the group, built my confidence. Every small risk helped me to get past the fear—which I believed to be a healing fear.

And it was.

During that time, I discovered a purpose I had not known, a burning desire to educate, inspire and empower. With every speech, it became more and more clear: My failure was a blessing that led me to my mission.

My boss, an incredible guy who understood my potential better than I did, had enough confidence in me to ask me to give an inspirational talk at a company meeting for our district. I wrote a short talk, which I rehearsed; I came prepared. This time, when I walked up to the podium, I felt no dread. This time, I was a bridled horse at the Kentucky Derby, waiting to be let out of the gate. By forging ahead, taking small risk after small risk, I went from thinking, *Do I really want to do this?* to *I can't wait to do this.*

That first big talk was a seminal moment in my life. For the first time, I could exhale. Suddenly, I knew that not only was I born to talk, but that I *could* talk. God had given me a voice that was pleasant to listen to, diction and vocabulary that were interesting to hear, and a purpose. My path was clear.

This is the ongoing controversy about the human being—is it nature or nurture that makes us who we are? A brother and sister can be raised in the same household, with the same value system,

**Success is inevitable if you answer
your call and stay the course.**

the same even-handed approach to the raising of each child by their mother and father, and can end up being two entirely different human beings. What is that? It's nature. It's DNA. Wiring. Staying the course was my wiring. It was my DNA, my unique gift.

God has put us here with a unique purpose. He assigned a job to you that only you can do, and if you do not do it, that job will not get done in the universe. To truly walk a successful, purposeful path, we must not ask, "What do I want from life?" No, there is only one question: "What does God want from me?"

You have to have the obedience to seek the answer to this question and then the personal discipline to do the work, to go through the pain and to stay the course. You are wired for your own mission. It's in your DNA; it is your unique gift. It will not be easy, but if it were easy, why would God need you? Success is inevitable if you answer your call and stay the course.

The hardest job a flower has is building its root base and getting down into the soil to suck out the nutrients it needs to grow. That's the hardest part of being a rose. The easiest part of being a rose is being a rose. So often, life is difficult for us, because we're not doing what God put us here to do. After it lays down roots, an oak tree will grow into the sky almost effortlessly, because an oak tree is not trying to be a weeping willow, just as a rose is not trying to be a carnation. Each of God's anointed living things is programmed to serve a particular purpose; all of nature knows this and acts (grows) accordingly.

Nature is not confused by this system; humans are confused. We are confused because all kinds of influences—mentors, parents, models, media—titillate us; veer us off our path; cause us to forget our wiring, our purpose, our job on this earth. When we are lost under these influences, our failures—epic or otherwise—serve as proof that we are not meant to do this all-important job. We falter. We give in. We give up. It's a huge mistake.

If I had given in to my fear of public speaking, if I had caved under the weight of failure and embarrassment, I would not have found myself years later, sharing a stage with a dream team of public speakers—Les Brown, Kweisi Mfume (former president and CEO of the NAACP) and T.D. Jakes—ready to educate, inspire and empower an audience full of hundreds of movers, shakers and decision makers.

Where once I could not speak, today I'm considered one of the most impactful speakers in America—knowledgeable, passionate and articulate in my subject matter expertise: networking, business and economic development. This is all because I found the blessing in failure and discovered my purpose.

The bright, steadfast, glorious entrepreneurs and speakers who co-authored this book with Les Brown and me, wrote *Mission Unstoppable: Extraordinary Stories of Failure's Blessings,* because they want you to rise up from your own perceived failures, from challenges that seem insurmountable, from disappointments that might crush your soul, and find your purpose.

My co-authors were chosen for this book because they had the courage to put their lives on blast to share something private and sometimes hurtful: to tell you about when it went wrong, what they learned and how they made it right. They are risk takers, people who are successful in their own right or who are on a trajectory of succeeding. They paid the price—they did the work, went through the pain and held on, even when the world seemed to be against them.

In this book, these remarkable individuals share their failures, but they also reveal strategies and tactics to help you stay the course. This is how we learn. This is how we grow. We locate ourselves in stories. Find yourself in their stories; in the pages of this book their truth is laid bare to show you the way home.

Chart a good and righteous course, and then stay that course. And all that is due you will come to you.

George C. Fraser is Chairman and CEO of FraserNet, Inc., a company he founded some twenty-eight years ago. Born in Brooklyn, NY, he was an orphan and foster child for fifteen years. He's written five best-selling books, including Success Runs in Our Race *and* Click. Upscale Magazine *named him one of the "Top 50 Power Brokers in Black America," and* Black Enterprise *magazine called him "Black America's #1 Networker." George has been featured on seven national magazine covers, and has received 350 awards and citations, including two honorary doctorate degrees and an African Goodwill Award. He's been married forty-two years and has two sons. Connect with George at Frasernet.com.*

LES BROWN

INTRODUCTION:
YOU'RE THE ONE

I don't know about your dream. I don't know how disappointed you've been working toward that dream. Here's what I *do* know about your dream: It's possible.

You may ask: Why am I certain your dream is possible? Because I do believe our dreams were given to us for the purpose of accomplishing those particular dreams. No matter what your background or circumstance; no matter who you are or where you come from; no matter if you dropped out of school, or failed to be true to yourself or lost your way; no matter if you failed, and failed and failed again; your dream is possible.

Growing up, I was labeled Educable Mentally Retarded. To say I struggled in school was an understatement. On paper, my future looked bleak. No one, save for my mother, Miss Mamie Brown, would have bet on me.

One day, just before finishing my junior year of high school, I received my report card. It indicated that I failed English and history and I would have to go to summer school. I was feeling down on myself, wondering why I seemed to be slower than everyone else, when I heard one of the teachers, Mr. Leroy Washington, giving a speech for graduating seniors in the auditorium. I wasn't supposed to be in there, but something told me I *had* to stay; something told me that speech was for me.

Mr. Washington said, "As a graduating senior of Booker T. Washington High School, I want you to know that you have the ability and the power to change the world, to transform people's lives, to live your dreams. And if just one of you can get the essence of what I've said, if just one of you can believe what I'm sharing with you now, my being brought here, in Miami, Florida, to Booker T. Washington High School, will not have been in vain."

As he spoke, my heart beat faster, and tears ran down my face.

"You can make your parents proud. You can make your school proud. You can touch millions of lives," he said, "and the world will never be the same because you came this way."

The world will never be the same because you came this way.

Your dream is possible.

Mr. Washington received a standing ovation. He left after the speech, and, clutching my report card in my hand, I ran after him.

I caught up with him in the parking lot and said, "Mr. Washington, do you remember me?"

"No," he replied.

"I'm Leslie Brown. My mother works in the cafeteria here," I said. "I've got these big dreams. I like talking to people. I like to make people feel good. I like to make them laugh. I want to be on the radio one day. Can I do that, sir?"

Mr. Washington looked at me and said, "It's possible."

As he walked away I said, "Mr. Washington—"

"What do you want now?"

"Mr. Washington, you said if one person here understands the essence of what you just said, that we have greatness in us, that we can change the world, that we can make our school proud and we can make our parents proud. I'm adopted, and I want to make my mother proud. Do you think I can do that?"

He said again, "It's possible," and turned to walk away.

"Mr. Washington!" I cried with tears streaming down my face. "I'm the one." Lips trembling, heart beating fast, I repeated, "I'm the one. You remember me, sir. I'm Miss Mamie Brown's boy. I'm the one. I'm the one.

It has been said that the two most important moments in our lives are the day we were born and the day we realized why we were born. Your dreams matter. My friend Joelle Martin once said, "What would the world be like if everyone lived their dreams?" After years of doing seminars and workshops and having the opportunity to hear people talk about their dreams—finding cures for cancer; ending world suffering, poverty, wars, hunger and homelessness—I believe that dreams are from God and all of us are sent here with an assignment to make our dreams become reality, to make the world a better place.

The great theologian and civil rights leader Howard Thurman, mentor to Dr. Martin Luther King, Jr., like Mahatma Gandhi and other leaders said, "There is something in every one of you that waits and listens for the voice of the genuine in yourself.

Life isn't a sprint; it's a marathon.

It is the only true guide you will ever have. And if you cannot hear it, you will all of your life spend your days on the ends of strings that somebody else pulls." Whatever you were called to do, whatever this "something" is for you, whatever your "genuine" is, you must draw your own line in the sand, take up the challenge and fight, fight, fight for your dream. Why? Because you're the one. You're the one to fulfill the promise of the dream God gave you.

Fighting for your dreams is not easy. We can predict the outcome of some dreams, but most of the time, *a dream has a life of its own*. When will a baby walk? He will walk when he walks. When will a baby talk? She will talk when she talks. We seldom know the day or the hour that our dreams will come true, which can make the whole thing seem just a bit *too* hard. We do all of this work pushing past comfort zones; setting aside fears; slaying inner demons; recommitting to the goal every day, every single day; and we *still* don't know when it will come to fruition. And most of the time, I can tell you based upon my own experience, you will fail your way to success.

Failure is not a destination; it's an invitation to unforeseen victories. Someone once said that a person who has never failed has never done anything. Make failure your vitamin. When you fail, especially when it hurts, be willing to pick yourself up, dust yourself off and get back in the game. Life isn't a sprint; it's a marathon. Are you in it to win it?

If you feel you "blew it," embrace that moment. Remember, it's just a memory. The past only exists in your mind. You have the absolute power to release it. Learn from it and then

Failure has not come to stay— it has come to pass.

let it go. There is a fundamental difference between failure and temporary defeat. If you learn from your failure and are able to move on from it—stronger, better, wiser, more determined—you haven't failed at all. You have merely graduated into a brand new opportunity to manifest your greatness. Be willing to fail your way to success!

When I look at life, I know that it's about the willingness to stand up; the willingness to fight for what you want; and the willingness not to deny a disease, hardship or circumstance, but rather, to defy it. It takes persistence, perseverance and a fighting spirit to achieve anything you want in life. Wilson Pickett had a song that was called, "99 and a Half Won't Do" and went on to say: You have to have one hundred. A.L. Williams, entrepreneur and motivational speaker, used to motivate his staff by saying, "All you can do is all you can do, and all you can do is enough. But make sure you do all you can do."

It is critical that you believe in yourself. Most of us don't have the courage or the willingness to say "yes" to our dreams, much less to stand up and fight for them—especially if we have "failed" along the way. This is partly because society tells us to focus on our limitations rather than on our potential. Eighty-seven percent of Americans go to jobs they hate. In the United States, the heart attack rate increases by thirty-five percent on Monday mornings between the hours of six and ten. The majority of these stressed-out, fear-driven individuals die on the toilet, getting ready to go to work someplace they hate. They focus on their limitations, rather than their possibilities, and then curl up and die. You must fight for your dreams as if your life depends on it, because it does.

If you've failed, remember that everything does not always happen when we want it to happen. Do not let delayed gratification or disappointment deter you from your dream.

The Chinese bamboo tree must be watered and fertilized every day. It takes five years of watering and fertilizing before the bamboo tree breaks through the ground. If at any time in

**A beautiful dream is growing
just under the surface.**

the nurturing process, the watering and fertilizing stops, the bamboo tree will die in the ground. Once it breaks through in that fifth year, the tree will grow ninety feet tall in six weeks! So, the question is, does the Chinese bamboo tree grow ninety feet in five years, or in six weeks? The answer is obvious: five years.

You may nurture your dream for years and see little or no movement, not realizing that it's growing where you cannot see it, not realizing that you are but a few years, months, days, or perhaps *moments* away from seeing it burst through and rise up, seemingly out of nowhere. In those years of growth, as you nurture your dream day in and day out, as you water and fertilize it and treat it with tender love, care and devotion, you may wonder if it truly is possible. Never forget what Mr. Leroy Washington said in his speech to graduating seniors, and to me in the parking lot later that day: It's possible.

God said, "You must have faith to call forth those things that be not as though they were." Judge not according to your circumstances, or based upon what you have now; do not fixate on the dirt on the ground. Remember, a beautiful dream is growing just under the surface.

If you are going through hard times, it's all right. Failure has not come to stay—it has come to pass. No matter how bad it is, or how bad it gets, you will make it. Put that message up on your bathroom mirror. Carry it in your wallet. Post it on your refrigerator. Say that affirmation every day; say it *several times a day*. "No matter how bad it is, or how bad it gets, I'm going to make it."

If you want to rise up and achieve a goal others have deemed impossible; if you want to overcome your perceived failures and disappointments and beat every last odd to realize the dream you've held in your heart for years, for decades, for a lifetime; if you want to step into greatness and meet your destiny, you must find that which will give you the courage to come back and try again and again and again.

What are your reasons? Why do you want this dream of yours? Why must you reach your goals?

You must take personal responsibility to make your dream happen. George Bernard Shaw said, "The people that make it in this world look around for the circumstances they want, and if they can't find them, they create them."

Every day for nineteen years, I get up in the morning. I hit the ground fighting cancer. My doctor at The Ohio State University, Dr. Monk, says that I'm God's miracle child. I guess I've been that all my life.

Over the years I've created products while in excruciating pain. Between the shots, my body would be sweating and trembling from the debilitating pain of cancer that's metastasized to seven areas of my body. I believe that I'm still here because I've been given grace.

I've come to know that life is a fight for territory, and once you stop fighting for what you want, what you don't want will automatically take over. The reason you picked up this book is because we're cut from the same cloth. We're branches of the same tree. There's something in your heart, in your DNA, that says to you that "You were born to win and quitting is not an option."

Coming from my background, labeled Educable Mentally Retarded, to become a world-renowned speaker who has motivated millions, I certainly faced failure, and I definitely had to create the circumstances and opportunities I needed to reach my dreams, to make good on my promise to myself and my mother and to fulfill my declaration to Mr. Washington all those years ago. I said it and meant it then, and I'll say it and mean it now: I'm the one. I know this for a fact. I've lived it.

Do you know what else I know for sure? *You're the one.* You are *only* one who can fulfill the dream God gave you. You. Only you. What does failure matter when you know this to be true?

Les Brown is a distinguished authority on harnessing human potential. A top motivational speaker, an extraordinary speech coach and the bestselling author of Live Your Dreams, It's Not Over Till You Win *and* Up Thoughts for Down Times *and co-author of the bestselling book* Fight for Your Dreams, *his passionate, straight-from-the-heart message motivates audiences to create a larger vision for their lives and to fight for their dreams.*

Born in an abandoned building in Liberty City, Florida and raised in poverty, Brown rose from a hip-talking morning DJ to become a thrice-elected state representative in Ohio, and then an award-winning, premier keynote speaker for Fortune 500 companies and for organizations worldwide. He is the recipient of the National Speaker Association's highest honors: the Council of Peers Award of Excellence. He also received the highest award from Toastmasters International: The Golden Gavel Award. Toastmasters International separately named him one of the top five speakers in the world. His PBS program You Deserve *was awarded a Chicago-area Emmy. Brown is now a radio personality at KFWB NewsTalk 980 AM in Los Angeles. He is also a communication and speech consultant who teaches people how to unwrap their "infinite greatness." Connect with Les at www.LesBrown. com and email him your personal success story.*

DENNIS KOLB

SILVER LININGS

In May of 2001, two weeks before my high school graduation, I was diagnosed with leukemia. I had already finished my advanced-placement courses and started local college classes at Mesa State University. I had, toured my future college campus at Northern Arizona University and planned my career: building on my aptitude for math, I would study to become an actuary. My bags were packed, my money was saved and I was ready to go.

The day before my diagnosis, my mom took me to see a doctor because I had been feeling fatigued. We'd seen a couple of doctors, but none of their solutions or treatments seemed to help with my exhaustion.

At this visit, the doctor said, "Your lymph nodes are swollen," and then took a few blood samples. "Things don't look good," he told us. "I'll be in touch tomorrow with the results."

That night, I contemplated if I might have cancer. My grandfather died of cancer and it terrified me, at first. I stayed up until three in the morning, sitting out in the cold, coudy Colorado night, looking into the snow-filled sky. *This could be my last night*, I thought. *What if it were*? I looked back at my life, at everything that had happened to me, and I realized, if this is the end, *I'm content with the life I've lived*. Despite the uncertainty of my looming diagnosis, it was one of the most peaceful moments of my life. Looking back on that moment I always think of the chorus in the song "Mad World" by Gary Jules, "I find it kinda funny, I find it kinda sad, the dreams in which I'm dying are the best I've ever had."

The next day, while I was getting ready for school, the doctor called before his office was scheduled to be open. He said, "You need to get to the emergency room right away."

At the hospital, the emergency room doctor said, "We've looked at your blood samples and we've concluded that you have a type of leukemia. We don't know which kind."

Leukemia. I'd been healthy my entire life; I had no idea what that was. I looked over at my mom, her eyes wide with shock. "Mom, are they saying I have leprosy?" I asked, not realizing leukemia was a form of cancer.

"Oh, honey," she replied. "How I wish it was."

"I just need a Gatorade," I said, my go-to drink when I felt tired. "And I need to get back to school." With no "senior ditch"

You have a type of leukemia.

days left, I was worried about how missing too many days of school would affect my graduation. I had a lot to do and I wanted to get on with my day!

The doctor looked at me and said, "You walked in with an extremely low red blood cell count. Normally, a person with a count this low would be unconscious."

That's crazy, I thought. *Yesterday I took an advanced-placement English test and got an A+!*

"We can't let you leave," the doctor continued. "We're getting a room ready for you."

"A room? I don't need a room," I said, unable to process why everyone was making such a big deal about it.

The nurse put a central IV line in my vein and sent me to my new hospital room. My family and friends had gathered, and that's when it finally hit home: I have cancer. I realized that, even though I may be content to pass on, my family was not prepared to let me go. I had to fight this battle—for them. They didn't know that just the night before I had come to terms with dying from cancer, but I certainly hadn't ever thought about how hard it would be on them to live without me around.

I had the world at my fingertips—I never thought I'd have to deal with a fatal illness until I was older.

As soon as it finally registered that I did in fact have cancer, suddenly that was the only thing on my mind. There was no future, and no past. From that moment on, I knew the negativity would certainly destroy me, if I let it. So instead, I resolved to have an optimistic mind, to only think of positive outcomes.

I turned to my family, their eyes full of fear and concern, and said, "Everything will be okay."

That next day, I did everything they say you should do to keep a positive mindset, including shaving my head so I wouldn't have to deal with my hair falling out after the chemotherapy treatments began.

I was overdosed with chemo the very next day. The adult dosage of chemo was too much for my eighteen-year-old body, and within hours I was vomiting profusely. The acidity from the vomit tore a hole in my esophagus, causing the yeast from my

I was overdosed with chemo the very next day.

throat to leak into my bloodstream, a systemic fungal infection which the doctor said was, "incurable." Because of the hole, every time I breathed, my chest cavity filled with air.

I was in agony, extemely terrified. I looked up at my mom and said, "Would you hug me?"

She did, and as she laid me back down said, "Dennis, you're not going *anywhere.*"

Eventually, the pain grew to be too much and I blacked out and went into shock. The body has a threshold for pain. When you experience more pain than your body can tolerate, your body will often make sure you aren't awake for it. When I awoke I was on life support. Even though the tear in my esophagus miraculously healed, I still had a fungal infection, so I had to be transported by Flight For Life to a new hospital. There another miracle happened; the FDA had just approved a drug specifically designed for my infection. These are just two miracles among many others that happened.

Due to the overdose, in the weeks that followed I had several close encounters with death. I lost a quarter of my body weight; I came dangerously close to total organ failure and lost most of my normal nerve function.

Every time I came off life support my mom said, "Well, honey, you're still here. God must have something planned for you."

Despite all of the pain and trauma, I was determined to keep my positive attitude. After one particularly scary close call, I said, "Mom, all is as it should be. Things are the way they are. If God wants them to be different, He'll make them different."

When I was released from the hospital—my high school diploma and cap and gown unopened—I was paralyzed from my voice box down. The doctor said I would probably never walk again. I had cheated death several times, but at a high cost.

I could have a *new* dream
and a *new* purpose.

I still had to face years of chemotherapy treatments as well as permanent liver and nerve damage. I suppose it would have been understandable if I fell apart after all that, but I knew that if I had a victim mentality, it would handicap me more than the paralysis and would pose a greater threat to my life than the cancer.

Even though I had earned a reason for others to pity me, somehow I knew that if I focused on how much pain I was in; or how traumatizing the experience in the hospital had been;

or how unlucky I was compared to my friends who were going off to college, their big bright futures spread out before them like the yellow brick road, I would just give all of the pain and disease more power.

I was bound and determined to walk again. I was not content in a wheelchair; a walker wouldn't do it either, and a life of dependency was not enough. I knew if there was someone in charge of my life, it was going to be me.

Being a statistics and probability guy, I knew that if I could get my doctors, nurses and other members of my medical team giggling, if I could get them into a good mood, the procedures

There is always a silver lining—always.

would be more successful. Logically, if I could influence their day in a positive way, they could perform better. So, I always made sure to focus on creating a lighthearted, fun atmosphere.

Every day—and on tough days, sometimes every hour—I looked for the silver lining in the situation. Every time I finished a surgery, I celebrated that I made it through. I didn't care if I had another one scheduled for the very next day, I still celebrated that I was healthy enough to have the surgery, that the surgery was successful, that I had lived to see another day.

I looked at all of my experiences, even those others would understandably label as "bad" experiences, as *good* experiences. I was sure I would be well, that I would recover, and so everything that happened along the way was just part of the journey leading me to a destination that I could not yet fully appreciate, for which I was certain the purpose would be revealed to me. Even if I had passed away, I had given it my best shot.

I had lost a lot—I couldn't play basketball, I couldn't have the career I planned for myself, or all of the dreams I imagined. But I could have a *new* dream and a *new* purpose. And I wasn't worried about what that would be. I knew my experiences would make me unique, and that was amazing. I kept my vision out of the future and out of the past and focused on the moment at hand.

When leukemia patients hit the five-year mark from the date of diagnosis, they are considered cured. About four months before the end of my three year, two month, chemo treatment, the doctor brought in a slide from one of my many painful bone marrow biopsies and said, "See, here? It's clear."

So I was well on my way. But I was also told the chemo overdose had severly compromised my liver to the point of failure.

"You can either continue with treatments for another four to six months and have a liver transplant," the doctor said, "or, you can stop treatment now, risking the cancer may return with no treatment options, and keep your liver."

I was twenty-two years old by this time, and opted to end treatments, keep my liver, and begin the healing process. With all the miracles I had experienced, I gained a new, improved optimistic mindset. *I had no more fear.* My doctor smiled; she agreed with my decision.

Today, I am thirty-two years old and cancer-free. I can walk. I still have some neuropathy in my legs and I'll probably never dunk a basketball again. I can do other things though—different things, things I never knew I would be interested in doing. I focus on what I can do and welcome new passions. I ignited a new spark of passion and purpose in my life, rather than bemoan the future I didn't get to have.

We continually lose dreams; it's part of life. Some of those losses are due to circumstances beyond our control; some are of our own doing. No matter how your dreams shift and change, you can rise above it and live beyond it. You can have a *new* dream. I told my mother in the hospital room, "All I have to do now is rise beyond my dreams."

The old dreams were fine and dandy, but what I'm doing now far surpasses their promise. With my Rise Beyond Dreams Foundation, I give back to people who are affected by life-threatening diagnoses and/or debilitating injuries. The Foundation serves as a beacon, bridging the gap between disease and trauma and a life of promise and passion. Along the journey I saw everything was as it should have been, and I gained the wisdom designed for me. I've found my purpose is to be a vessel for those who are overwhelmed by a traumatic event, like myself and everyone who was affected, creating a community filled with courage, hope and the discovery of new passions.

It's easy to get caught up in the "why me" trap when you're faced with a crisis or dealing with failure or loss. When I was diagnosed, a lot of people asked that very question: "Why, Dennis?" I thought about it; I let those questions run around in my mind. *Why me? Why do I have it so bad?* And then I asked myself, *Whom would I rather it be in my shoes? Whom would I give this cancer to instead? My mother, my father, or sister— maybe my grandmother or aunts, uncles, cousins, friends?* The answer always is the same: no one. I know my strengths and what I can handle. I was given these experiences for a reason. What I learned was, blessings come in many disguises.

When you feel overwhelmed, harness that moment; look outside of yourself and focus on the silver lining. If you can do that, overcoming the obstacle becomes secondary.

Know there is always a silver lining—always. Dr. Linda Stork, the doctor who took over my care after the chemo overdose, was so moved by my story she decided to leave her position at the hospital and dedicate her research to young people with cancer. You see, part of the issue with the overdose was, while there were protocols for chemotherapy dosages for children under eighteen, and for adults over twenty-two, there were no specific protocols for youth *between* the ages of eighteen and twenty-two.

Dr. Stork said, "This can't happen again. I'm going to move to a research hospital in Oregon and work specifically on what I've seen happen with you, Dennis."

Today, I'm proud to say there is an international protocol for chemotherapy dosages for eighteen to twenty-two-year-old cancer patients. Think of how many young people with cancer will be saved from the life-threatening and permanent effects of a chemotherapy overdose? Wouldn't you consider that to be a silver lining?

Whatever trauma, failure, crisis or disappointment you've experienced, remember it is just a life event—it does not own you. You are in charge of your future. More importantly, the life event you experienced, however difficult, has many a silver lining that you may not yet see, but they are surely there: a new you, the you that God intended you to be.

Even when the outcome is grim, stay persistent, stay optimistic and have faith that every experience is meant to make you stronger and more appreciative of the things you may have taken for granted.

There is always a way to find your silver linings. *Always.*

Dennis Kolb is the founder of Rise Beyond Dreams, a nonprofit organization serving people facing life-threatening diagnoses and debilitating injuries and their loved ones. Through a free membership site and "Alumni" workshops, Rise Beyond Dreams helps people support their bodies' innate ability to heal, re-ignite their passions despite the challenges of ongoing medical treatment, form lifelong bonds and enduring relationships through social experience and ultimately build better futures after diagnosis.

A professionally-trained motivational speaker from Les Brown's "Circle of Mastery" program, Dennis speaks about his journey from an academic/athlete just days away from his high school graduation to a young man not only fighting leukemia, but the disastrous effects of an overdose of chemotherapy. Dennis's story is an inspiration to anyone facing a life-altering challenge. Connect with Dennis at www. RiseBeyondDreams.org.

"L" "C" GREEN, JR.

THE RIGHT FIT

Around the corner from my childhood home in Blytheville, Arkansas lived one of the greatest role models of my life, Mr. John-John. Everyone in town knew him. He owned a teenage cafe—essentially a soda shop where we kids would spend whatever money we had—a cafe for adults, a pool hall and a small hotel.

I was tall for my age, sort of fooled adults into thinking I was older than I really was and, because of that, I was able to get into the pool hall when my friends would be turned away. I liked going there for reasons besides the obvious; there I had my very first job. A man could play a table for ten cents a game back then. One day, when I was about twelve, Mr. John-John whistled me over. He pointed to a piece of paper with scratches on it and a pile of dimes.

"I need you to count those dimes," he said, "and make sure they're the same number as on that paper."

At the time I didn't think anything of it. I counted them up and told him they matched, and then we went to the bank so that I could make sure they came up with the same amount. But at the end of that first bank transaction, I noticed Mr. John-John signed his signature with an X. He couldn't read or write.

How on earth could one of the most successful men in our town run four businesses without those basic skills? I made a joke of it to my mother later on, and she got onto me. "That man owns more of Arkansas than just about anybody," she scolded, "so he knows *something*."

I learned that lesson quickly: Never disrespect anyone, because you have no idea what they're capable of achieving.

Success doesn't always come with airplanes and flashy boats; sometimes it comes in unexpected ways. My grandmother was a sharecropper. When I was a child, I loved helping pack that cotton up for storage since I didn't have to do it day in and day out! Sharecroppers take home forty percent of what their crop sells for, since they don't own the land. Now, my grandmother was pretty smart. She fenced off a little portion of that land where the cotton didn't grow and there she planted tomatoes, corn, peas, you name it. She knew to leave some chickens and ducks there to eat the bugs and keep from needing any pesticides. Everything in that little patch of land she got to keep, all one hundred percent of it. And it earned interest, too! Eggs and meat from the birds, and those vegetables paid for themselves time and again since their seeds could be used to plant the next year's crops.

It may seem simple to some folks, but I like to use that as an example of how to diversify your income. That's smart business planning. She had to walk a mile to work that garden, then a mile home, arms loaded down with the fruits of her labor. And she did

Don't let people tell you that you can't have money or success.

that day in and day out, managing all of this on her own. She did well and she was another excellent role model for me to see how wealth and a heavy workload can be managed.

When most people think of Arkansas in the 1950s, they don't think of Black people's wealth, especially not of their having been successful. But in my town, that was our reality. Our grocer, Gus Walls, loaned money to the banks that had failed during the Great Depression. The dentist from our side of town did, too. Every business on my block was owned by a Black family. Everyone was meeting their needs and doing well for themselves. The world at that time may not have had faith in us, but we didn't know anything but to do our best. I came up with Black businesses around me and I was taught to respect that achievement. Don't let people tell you that you can't have money or success.

School and I did not get along at first. There were many times I didn't want to go and, quite frankly, I failed the seventh grade. Twice. After that, I decided no more for me. I waited until I was seventeen so I could join the Navy. It was the start of the Vietnam War, and I figured the Navy was a better bet than the Army. Their uniforms were sharp, too. I failed the entrance exam to get into the Navy three times, but finally I passed.

It turned out that I wasn't a good fit for the Navy, either. After boot camp, we were shipped off; ultimately we landed on Naval Air Station Guam for air support, where I was trained to be a firefighter. It seems I had my own way of doing things, and that's not really

Our attitude toward life is what determines life's attitude toward us.

what they're looking for in the Navy. An airplane crashed on the runway, and my job was to get the trapped pilot out before the plane exploded. I was told to cut his leg off to get him out and I wasn't going to do that.

Instead, I cut the surrounding metal and straps, unfortunately dislodging a bomb, which clanged to the tarmac, sending everyone scrambling. I laughed, because if it hadn't gone off when it fell, it wasn't going to go off at all. I managed to get the pilot out of there whole and hale, but disobeying orders meant I was sent to work with the Seabees doing grunt work.

The world was trying to tell me that I wasn't fit for much. Good thing I wasn't listening. After four years and eight months in the Navy, I was honorably discharged with a G.I. Bill good for a hundred and thirty dollars a month in school allowance. I only had a sixth grade education, but I didn't think there would be any harm in trying to go to college. I applied at the local community college, Long Beach City College. Not even an hour after applying, I got a phone call telling me I was accepted.

First trying to take classes in heating, ventilation and air conditioning, so I could learn a trade, I was rejected by the instructor because I dressed too nicely for that sort of dirty work. It was suggested that I take regular classes instead, possibly political science courses, so I signed up for those.

It turns out that I was a great fit for higher education. I can remember going into the administration offices to get my first set of grades, fully expecting it to be D's. To my surprise, I had a row of B's and C's. I was a guy who had flunked out of seventh grade, shuttled around from job to job, and there in my hand was proof that up until then, I just hadn't found what was right for *me*.

After that first report card I applied myself even more, challenging myself to do better. I became wholly immersed in learning, in the environment at the school. I joined the student

Stop being afraid of making mistakes.

council and even became student body president. A few young ladies approached me to help create a Black Students' Union, of which I eventually became president.

I'd gone to college thinking that I couldn't be anything more than a tradesman—not that there's anything wrong with that work. But I was ready to do something more—realizing that I *could* be more. I could be a teacher or a political scientist, a director of a social justice program, anything I could imagine. Everything that I'd been made to believe about myself was false.

I applied to the University of California, Irvine and was accepted, not just by the school, but also by my fellow students. I had learned something from old Mr. John-John: If you don't tell people what you can't do, they'll only know what you can do. No one needed to know I once flunked out of grade school, because there I was proving that I had what it takes. I graduated from

California State University, Dominguez Hills with a degree in political science with a behavioral science minor.

The single most important factor that guarantees success is a healthy attitude. Our attitude toward life is what determines life's attitude toward us. My parents always made me believe I could do anything or be anyone I wanted to be. My dad would point out every successful businessman in our little town and tell me all the ways they'd fought the odds and become who they were; he made me understand how important it was to know that where you come from, the challenges you're faced with in life, none of that will stop anyone who is determined to excel.

I saw Mr. John-John one time after leaving the Navy, but we didn't stop to talk. I've thought about him over the years, how he had what others would call serious limitations on his ability to

Don't be afraid of what you don't know.

succeed, and yet he owned half the town. At one time he even had a former Staff Sergeant from the Army, a man with a PhD, working for him. Anything was possible, that's what I learned from that man.

You can achieve success no matter the condition of your life. You have to want it, you have to work for it and, most importantly, you have to not be afraid to try. You have to have the drive, the desire and the belief that you can do it. You have to stop being afraid of making mistakes, because you're going to make them. Everyone does. Learn from them and keep pushing forward.

Don't be afraid of what you don't know, either. Skills can be taught, knowledge can be learned, but you can't experience success if you don't put forth the effort. An old friend of mine, Les Brown, once told me, "You can sit on the bank of the river and read books all day long on how to swim; until you jump out there and swallow about half that river, you're not going to learn."

When I was young and failing grade school, I didn't know what was available for me to do, didn't know all the possibilities. What

I was being taught didn't fascinate me, and so I didn't try. And I failed because I didn't try. But I tried to get into the Navy, then I tried one more time to get an education, and it worked. College challenged me in a way I hadn't been challenged before. It was exciting; it was a world I hadn't known existed.

Don't give up. Maybe you just haven't found what fits you best, yet, but you won't know what does fit if you don't put yourself out there and try.

"L" "C" Green, Jr. is the founder of LC Green & Associates, Inc., a company that has provided tax accounting and financial management services for more than thirty years. He is also a qualified provider of education for all tax professionals, has been an instructor at three colleges in Los Angeles County, and is a loan intermediary with the Small Business Administration. He was awarded the Constant Contact Small Business of 2013 Award for Social Media, has written numerous articles and has published eight books with topics ranging from marketing principles to tax preparation and to principles of financial control. Connect with "L" "C" at www.LCGreen.com or www.facebook.com/ LCGreenBooksForSuccess.

STAN RICHARDS

LEARN, EARN AND RETURN

I drive in my Bentley down the streets where I once lived, each block in the projects the same jungle of three-story beige apartments crowded against each other, lined with chain-link fences, broken-down cars and kids on the corner trying to hustle for a living. These are streets where I used to stand and dream of something bigger for myself, something much better than this.

In this moment, as I sit in luxury, with my beautiful wife Chereace and our two handsome sons waiting for me back in our large and well-appointed home, I know my belief that I could achieve it, my faith that my God would help me if I helped myself, my perseverance even when it was hard, has paid off. The rules for success have worked. I come back to these same hard streets to help lift up the impoverished citizens of my old community, proof that life can be better, my heart full with appreciation and gratitude for what I've been able to achieve.

Instability is the best word to describe my childhood. My wonderful mother was raising six children in the projects of Washington, D.C. in the 1970s and did the best she could for us. But as many people who grow up on government assistance know, it's not always enough. We'd eat great at the first of the month, then struggle to find enough to eat until payday rolled around again the next first of the month.

It was hard out there, not just to make a living, but to *live*. Most of my peers didn't have goals. They didn't aspire to anything greater than to make it through to the end of the day. I can remember being ten years old thinking to myself, "I'm going to be a millionaire." A lot of kids have thought that, but I actually achieved it. It wasn't easy—nothing worthwhile ever is—but I achieved it by seeing something bigger than my narrow surroundings.

I looked around at what we had—and it wasn't much!—and imagined more. I knew that I wanted to get out of the "'hood." I wanted a good job with a steady paycheck, my own place and a

Most of my peers didn't have goals.

nice ride. I believed that because I could visualize where I wanted to go, I would be able to get there. After all, how can you follow a path if you can't see it? To succeed, you have to visualize where you're going, picture that future you've always wanted for yourself.

Most people can't see past their noses. If you don't have a vision or an idea of where you'll go in your life, you'll end up anywhere. In other words, don't live life by chance. I envisioned myself as unstoppable and capable of doing whatever I put my mind to. There's a saying: "Once the mind expands, it will never be the same." My expanded vision allowed me to see a world that I never knew existed, one full of tremendous possibility.

An ounce of discipline outweighs a ton of regret. One of the keys to my success was learning how to be disciplined. I sure didn't have that modeled for me growing up. I did what I wanted, went to school or stayed home as I pleased and stayed out as long as I desired. There were no rules, at least in my mind. You can imagine the shock I had when I entered the workplace. *I have to be on time?* I can laugh at that now, but back then I didn't realize that having a job wasn't just about me; other people were depending on me as well. I quickly learned that in order to keep a job, let alone start climbing that ladder, I was going to have to buckle down and learn how to focus, how to keep pushing myself to do better.

My life's trajectory changed drastically in 2005 when my brother Tim was diagnosed with pancreatic cancer. I like to say that at this time I was institutionalized at my job—I was working one hundred hours a week driving a bus in those same projects I'd moved away from, just to chase money. When my brother was diagnosed, I had a pattern interrupt. Instead of every day being the same, constantly working to provide for my family, I realized that I wasn't enjoying it. I wasn't able to, not working those hours!

Instead, I asked myself, "What am I doing here? My life now is about my job, not about my family and enjoying any quality time with them."

I had the discipline, I had a vision, but I realized that I needed to position myself around people who would inspire me to stay on my path, people who were achieving their own goals, people I could aspire to be like. I realized early that you are the sum total of the five people you hang around most. Most of my friends made a

An ounce of discipline
outweighs a ton of regret.

hundred thousand dollars yearly after working hours of overtime. I like to call them hundred-thousand-aires! Nothing was wrong with that, but I realized if I was going to the next level in business and in life, I would need to begin hanging around people who were where I wanted to be and had the lifestyle I wanted.

I realized that I needed to do something different and I needed change in my life. So I joined the direct sales company 5LINX. My wife and I became a team working toward a goal of success and peace, one of gratitude and thankfulness. I truly believe that was the missing piece in my life's vision.

My relationships with the co-founders and other leaders in the company allowed me to dream bigger and expand my vision and level of thinking. These relationships helped me step outside of my comfort zone. I've learned that success is usually waiting for us when we step beyond what's comfortable. I've learned so much in the last several years just by positioning myself with the right people. It's helped me expand my vision of what's possible. We must stop hanging out with folks who don't share our goals. Once you position yourself around the right people, ask how they got to where they are and how you can do it.

Nothing in your life has meaning if you don't give it meaning. I want people to understand how important it is to connect with something bigger than ourselves. I could say how much I loved and cherished my family, but when I was working all the time, keeping myself from them, was I cherishing my family? I needed a mental pattern interrupt.

True living is when you're giving and serving. Making a million dollars is great, don't get me wrong, but I know now that you get true gratification from giving and serving your community. Add value to the planet, to the people around you. What you can do to connect with something beyond yourself is set small goals to start with, get that small taste of accomplishment. This will lead you to your passion and your passion will lead you to your purpose.

I want the blue-collar folks—the sanitation workers, taxi drivers and barbers, just to name a few—to know that your job is not the end all! Don't let yourself or others define you by your job, position or title. You can still develop your own wealth. Think outside the box! Write that love story. Record that song you've been singing to yourself all these years. Complete that invention you had in mind. Embrace your fears. Right beyond your fear you'll find your success. My small goal was starting a business, which led to me speaking around the country—something I love—which led to my purpose, The Richards Group Foundation.

This is one of the most important lessons I try to teach the youth through my foundation, which I named after my "shero" mother, Doris Olivia Richards. We strive to help underprivileged youth see a new vision for themselves, something beyond simply making it to the end of the day.

If I thought I had it tough in the projects back in the 1970s, it's nothing compared to how hard it is for these kids today. The youth with whom I work, mostly young women between the ages of eleven and sixteen—and we're always ready for the young men of the neighborhood to join us, too!—come from broken homes. They're poor, they're undereducated, they're surrounded by drugs and gangs and negativity. The world they live in seems pretty limiting.

Now, when I drive my Bentley through my old neighborhood on my way to work with the youth who benefit from The Richards Group Foundation programs, I wonder how I'll get through to the kids that day. It took me a few visits to realize that these kids

**Nothing in your life has meaning
if you don't give it meaning.**

couldn't tell me what their dreams were for themselves—they had none! All they were doing was surviving day-to-day. How can they possibly dream of a better life when the only life they *know* is one of failure, fear and disappointment?

The Richards Group Foundation helps them see what is waiting for them, how much more they can achieve, helps them see a new possible future; they just have to position themselves with people who can uplift their minds and inspire them to work hard, and then stay focused on achieving success.

If they set the goal of making the honor roll, I then ask, "What will you study next year?"

They set a goal for graduation, and I ask, "Which college do you think you might want to attend?"

They want a business degree? "Excellent! What's the name of your future company?"

I want them to picture the path all the way to that last dream of a future filled with everything they could want.

Passion is great, but purpose is where your life becomes something extraordinary. When you're making a difference, the things that would derail you—the obstacles in your family and workplace, your surroundings, self-esteem issues—all fall away

35

when it's no longer just about you, but about something bigger than you. If you're just focused on personal wealth, it won't mean as much as if you were focused on that and then helping others get that, too. Service is a beautiful thing. Service fills your soul; service gives you purpose. Let service lead you to that final destination, an exceptional lifestyle that's fulfilling and gratifying.

You have to have faith, focus and action. Believe with a burning desire that you can accomplish anything you want if you really put your mind to it. I'm an example of what's possible: You *can* go from the bus to a Bentley. It's not about your background or where you come from. I believe we're all born great. The world and our experiences shape us and can put limitations on us. So don't let them. Take action to work toward your goals. Remember: A failure is someone who quits before the journey ends. Until you're living the life you've envisioned for yourself, for your family, and especially for your community, the journey isn't over.

Stan Richards is proof that you can do whatever you put your mind to. Despite the many hardships he faced, Stan graduated from high school and worked for the Federal Bureau of Investigation and the Washington Metropolitan Area Transit Authority. Stan honed his business strengths by teaching himself the ins and outs of entrepreneurship, creating the successful company, the Positive Black Men Coalition (PBMC) in 1992. Stan and his wife Chereace embarked on a new business venture, 5LINX, allowing Stan to share his business expertise with others. Quickly reaching a top position, double platinum senior vice president, Stan has also helped elevate six platinum senior vice presidents and sixty-seven senior vice presidents. He's published an autobiography, From the Bus to the Bentley: No More Limits, *detailing his steps for success.*

Stan established The Richards Group Foundation (www. TheRichardsGroupFoundation.org) to provide scholarships, events and resources to youth in an effort to empower them to see beyond the limits of their circumstances and dream bigger. For his vision and service to youth in his community, Stan was the recipient of the 2013 and 2014 Steve Harvey Ford Neighborhood Award for Best Community Leader.

When not fulfilling his many speaking engagements across the country, he spends his time with his wife Chereace and their two children, Stanley and Isaiah. Connect with Stan at his website: www. StanRichardsOnline.com.

SARAH GROSS

HAND OVER HAND

The ice axe strapped to my climbing partner's back started to hum as the storm rolled in. While he frantically tried to climb up to where I had set the belay, his eyes were as big as saucers. It was almost directly overhead, and we needed to get out of there.

We were close to a summit, high up in the Chamonix mountain range. I could see the top, but knew we wouldn't reach it with the storm rolling in. *Heck, we'll be lucky at this point to get off the mountain in one piece,* I thought. The temperature was dropping fast, and I could smell the charge in the air. "Crap," I murmured to myself, watching the dark clouds roll in fast.

I wasn't sure if it was going to be just the icy rain that was beginning to fall or eventually snow as well, but either way, I knew for sure there was lightning coming. A few strikes had just hit peaks close by, and I was nicely perched on top of the mini summit that lay beneath the main summit—a perfect target for one of those lightning strikes.

To make matters worse, I had all sorts of metal climbing gear clipped to my pack and my harness. *Why isn't this stuff made of plastic?* I wondered desperately. *Maybe then it wouldn't be humming and calling in the lightning for an up-close and personal visit.*

"Well, at least I don't have my ice axe with me," I muttered. Unfortunately for my climbing partner Miguel, I was leading the climb, so he was stuck carrying our "team" ice axe. It jutted up over his helmet, pointing straight toward the sky: a short, but fully functional lightning rod.

"It's humming and vibrating—we need to get out of here!" he yelled, his panic level obviously escalating.

Just then, the two Frenchmen who had been weaving over our rope all day arrived, each with an axe strapped to his back as well—three lightning rods were now jutting up toward the sky on the small peak we all were clinging to, each negotiating with the lightning above to see which could curry favor.

While waiting for Miguel to climb up to me, I'd tried to come up with an escape plan. The rock was now getting wet—climbing on dry rock isn't easy, but climbing on slick rock with cold hands and wet shoes is nearly impossible. I'd determined that the best option was probably to rappel down the short cliff about fifty feet below, where there seemed to be a small rock roof and a small patch of dirt.

"Not perfect, but we'd at least be protected from the wind and precipitation on two sides and potentially have some overhead cover," I told Miguel.

He and the Frenchmen agreed that that seemed to be the lesser of two evils. We all rappelled on one rope for speed and stowed our metal gear as far away from our four-by-four-foot patch of earth as

I knew for sure there was lightning coming.

possible. The rock roof was an apparition—there really wasn't one, and we had very little protection from the icy rain. I crouched into a ball and pulled my rain jacket over my knees to try to keep warm and to keep my legs and shoes as dry as possible.

As I sat balancing on my pack, grasping my shins and shivering, I had plenty of time to stew about our predicament. I'd studied the route and the approach the day before, had an accurate map of the route and had made sure we had the right gear. We had climbed efficiently, but we had made a critical mistake. We had put ourselves in this position before we even got *started. We didn't start early enough.*

I knew we should have started at least an hour earlier. Yes. I knew better. Even though the weather forecast was pretty good, there was a chance of storms in the late afternoon. Things can go wrong in the mountains, and weather can come in early. Case in point.

It took me a while to refocus and remind myself that I'd had a choice. Though Miguel had been adamant about leaving later so he could catch breakfast at his hotel, he didn't force me to get a late start. I went of my own free will. I could have chosen to say, "I'm

You need to focus on making small steps.

sorry, Miguel, but I don't wish to go on the climb if we get that late a start." Yes, I'd had the choice and I had chosen poorly. I was responsible for my current circumstances.

The weather broke after about a half hour. We couldn't wait long for the rock to dry, as we needed to get out of there before dark, and we had quite an adventure ahead. This section of the cliff wasn't on our maps, and no known route or rappel descent existed. Knowing that it appeared to be a difficult climb that had to be tackled with care but speed, we had to assess who was going to be the leader for what had become our group of four.

I was hoping that one of the well-seasoned Frenchmen would volunteer since we were on their home turf, but they stated that it should be the strongest technical climber since the route looked difficult. We eventually figured out that I was the strongest technical climber—in theory, at least. This meant I was on lead. *Great. The day just keeps getting better.*

As I prepared to head out onto the exposed wall, I centered my thoughts, focused on my breathing and reminded myself that progress is made one move at a time. If you focus on the unknowns and just wanting to reach the end, you get yourself out of the moment and out of the flow. Instead, the most efficient way to climb is to focus on how to solve each mini-problem you encounter and how to do each move most efficiently.

If you look too far out, you can't see all of the holds and features anyway. You then just start thinking about how impossible it seems and thoughts of failure or falling pop into your head. You start to over-grip and become unnerved.

If instead you focus on where you think you need to place your next piece of protection or where your next good rest stance will likely be and set that as your immediate target, then you are simply moving from mini-goal to mini-goal. It isn't as daunting, and it

Focus on what you can do.

allows you to focus on the basics: breathing, staying relaxed and how to make the next move most efficiently. This is the strategy I used as I made my way across the overhanging face with a thousand feet of air below me. Breathe, relax, focus on what is available.

In climbing, one of the biggest hurdles is getting over the fear of falling. Your comfort zone is being close to the ground and/or being close to your protection. To reach the top, though, you have to be able to break through the fear and make progress despite it. To do this you need to focus on making small steps, forcing yourself farther and farther outside of your comfort zone.

It was slow going: hand over hand, foot over foot. Seven years of climbing experience had taught me to be cautious, but at the same time to be willing to take calculated risks. With each move, more of the next part of the rock revealed itself. And, amazingly, holds materialized just as I needed them. What appeared as a blank, intimidating face from a distance was actually a beautiful line through breathtaking scenery. Probably no one had ever set foot on this part of the Alps before, and while it wasn't what we planned, it turned out to be an incredible adventure and privilege to be the first to venture on this spectacular route.

When we finally came upon the rappel anchors of a charted route, relief rushed through me. While the descent was far from over, we'd found our safety net. Being able to sit and take stock—not only of our situation, but also of the beautiful panoramic view we were at last able to truly appreciate—was heady and dizzying.

Some might be asking, "Why is this story in a book about how to succeed? Didn't you fail to reach the summit?" Good question. I tell this story here and to my students at CrushTheCubicle.com and FlexWorkFinder.com, because it reveals many powerful and universal success lessons.

Here are a few:

First, reaching your goals and achieving success is each person's own responsibility. What you think and how you react to your circumstances has a dramatic impact on your ability to overcome challenges and determines your ultimate level of success. If you

Step into your corridor of possibility.

focus on complaining, blaming and/or thinking about how difficult or scary things seem, you're just wasting your precious energy and resources. You're already dooming yourself to failure.

Instead, focus on what you can do. When you start focusing on what you can do and start taking action—even if it's only small steps toward your goal and even if you're scared or uncertain—that's when you step into the corridor of possibility. That's when you eventually achieve success beyond your dreams.

Take my community of those who are "Crushing The Cubicle" and recreating their lifestyles and careers to find more time and freedom. If they simply focused on complaining about their lack of freedom or how they wished they could spend more time with their loved ones or travel more, and never took steps to improve their situations, they would forever be stuck. They would be doomed to live a life without time, without adventure and without the freedom they crave.

Ask yourself, "Am I taking responsibility and taking action to make my dreams come true? Or am I simply hoping, wishing or worse yet, complaining about my current lot?"

Another big lesson is: Don't be afraid to fail and know it's probably never as bad or as scary as what you imagine. Now, I'm not advocating being reckless. Just as I climb with a rope and protection and have backup plans, you should also put measures in place to minimize your risks. Yet eventually you have to step out into the unknown. It may be scary; your heart may pound; your palms may get a little sweaty, but know you can handle whatever comes your way. After all, that's when you know you are growing—that you are living. And that's, as they say, "Where the magic happens."

Ask yourself, "What's the worst that could happen?" Then, ask yourself, "What can I do to minimize the risks? Can I handle it if it doesn't work out?" I bet you'll surprise yourself with your answers.

Lastly, this story shows that "failure" can often bring a new kind of success that you never even imagined, whether that's learning life lessons, acquiring new skills or opening a door to a new possibility that you never even knew existed or thought possible.

If my partner and I had never set our sights on that summit that day, we'd never have been in the position to find that hidden climb that lay undiscovered for thousands of years.

So, start… start on your adventure, step into your corridor of possibility and be open to the hidden opportunities that are just waiting to be discovered.

Sarah Gross is an international-award-winning business and marketing professor, entrepreneur, author, speaker, consultant and rock-climbing guide. Her current mission is to help one million people recreate their lifestyles and careers to find more time and freedom. To achieve this mission, she founded FlexWorkFinder.com and CrushTheCubicle.com. FlexWorkFinder.com is a jobsite that contains a proprietary database of flexible jobs, including telecommuting positions. CrushTheCubicle. com offers flexible career and business training. You can claim a free FlexWorkFinder membership, a Crush The Cubicle Starter Kit and over eleven thousand dollars in free gifts at FlexWorkFinder.com/les.

HAKI AMMI

AWAKENING

One hundred books. Every year, for eleven years, I read at least one hundred books a year. Two books one week, three another, I read books on economics, history, personal development, business and sociology. I read the classics. I read the great books by and about the thinkers and leaders of our time. I read all of the books I should have read in school, filling in the gaps, and hundreds of books that were not offered in school, expanding my horizons. I was on a quest. A quest for knowledge.

Over the course of eleven years I read more than eleven hundred books. Not bad for an "original gangster" who had to repeat the tenth grade.

Most who knew me when I began my quest would have assumed it had everything to do with a life-changing book I read at the recommendation of my brother. It's true; Haki Madhubuti's book *Black Men, Obsolete, Single, Dangerous?* opened my eyes to my own power, to my own truth. When he said, "I'm down with the Black Man Rising" it was the first time I realized I didn't have to be defined by the insane environment I grew up around, I didn't have to become another negative statistic.

And yes, it was Madhubuti's assertion that "reading should be like eating and sleeping" that inspired me to commit to reading two to six hours a day. But while powerful beyond measure,

Madhubuti's insights and ideas were only part of what compelled me to read one hundred books a year. Really, it began when I realized there was a whole world of information I did not know.

Depending on whom you ask, when most people tell you what Baltimore, Maryland is known for, they come up with the same few references: Johns Hopkins Hospital, the Baltimore Ravens, Thurgood Marshall and Harriet Tubman among them. These are positive organizations and role models that have inspired many young people toward greatness. But growing up in Baltimore, I wasn't conscious of that. I didn't know about the accomplished people and entities from my hometown. I knew the streets.

By the time I was seventeen years old, I was part of the city's drop-out statistic—only three out of ten freshmen graduated with their class. I hadn't officially dropped out, but I certainly wasn't going to school full time. My parents instilled me with good

I read at least one hundred books a year.

values, including getting my high school diploma, but I was too focused on being cool and hanging with my friends to heed their advice. I experienced a few minor brushes with the law, but since I avoided "real crimes," I thought my petty criminal behavior would not affect my life. *I'm too slick for that,* I thought.

One fateful night in 1991, all of that changed. I was outside a nightclub at two in the morning with my crew. In the parking lot was a harder, more street-entrenched crew that had a beef with some of the people I grew up with. One of their leaders walked up to us and started talking tough.

Then, he called me out by name and said, "You look like the tough one. What do you have to say?"

I didn't say a word. I swung. My punch surprised the leader so much that he fell to the ground. I hit him a few more times before one of the older members of my crew pulled out a .45 semi-automatic gun and fired a warning shot in the air. Fortunately, no one was killed or even injured; it could have turned into an ugly scene. All around me was commotion and chaos as we scrambled to pile into our cars and get away.

That night I couldn't sleep. My friends thought I should stay somewhere other than home, but even knowing no one could find me didn't calm my anxiety. My heart wouldn't stop pounding. I was terrified. Later, I learned the hardcore crew we fought with had swarmed my neighborhood looking for me, dressed in black and wearing ski masks like hit teams, armed with Uzis, Tech 9s and semi-automatic weapons. It was then that I knew: Life is not a game.

This is not shoplifting from the grocery store; this is not joyriding. I realized the lines between petty crimes and dangerous crimes were blurred and finally took stock. I knew some of the people in my

I thought my petty criminal behavior would not affect my life.

community had evolved from "juvenile" offenders into hardcore killers and drug dealers. If I kept up with my own behavior, what made me think I would escape that fate?

That night at the club was my first awakening. I decided right then and there to stop associating with anyone who committed crimes, petty or otherwise. *You need a future.* The very next day I made up my mind to get back into school.

One thing was very clear to me: I needed education. I did not know my options in the world. I did not know the trappings of the world, and because of that, on some level I had become a victim of my environment. I had to frame my own mindset, my own direction and my own path to begin to separate my mind from my physical environment that was so negative and destructive. It was the beginning of my mental evolution, the beginning of my new identity, the dawn of my purpose.

Little by little, day-by-day, class-by-class, my mind expanded. I felt empowered for the first time in my life, and unlike during my days on the street, I began to understand what invincible really felt like. After taking accelerated classes in order to catch up to my class, I made the honor roll in my senior year. And, even though I did not receive credits, I audited additional classes toward the end of high school. No longer would I be a victim of what I did not know.

Just a few years later, I read Madhubuti's book. He is not just a great thinker and author, but also a poet. His words synchronized with my spirit and encouraged me to look at myself as a man, to ask questions about the world I live in and to make a claim that I be free from the effects of my environment forever.

I made the declaration: Take control. Take ownership. Take responsibility. Take power over your destiny.

I began my quest for knowledge in earnest. "Reading should be like eating and sleeping" was my mantra. In 1993 I joined the United States Navy. I worked at a desk job, which had a lot of down time. I filled every bit of it with reading. I read Frederick Douglas,

Never let lack of knowledge hold you back.

Malcolm X and George Subira. Subira taught me about Black economics, which shifted my views. Malcolm's story of reading the dictionary inspired me to read a financial dictionary, cover to cover. That Douglas learned how to read by clipping articles from newspapers he found confirmed what I had been thinking: *I need to become an excellent reader.*

I began to understand the world through history books and literature. I began to build ideas, and wisdom, taking great interest in authors who came from backgrounds like mine. *If they came from the same environment, I could accomplish the same things.* Inspired, I began to focus on particular areas of my personal development that I knew needed enhancement and empowerment.

My desk was full of books, my room held stacks upon stacks of more books and I kept many books back home in Baltimore. During the five-and-a-half years I was in the military, I became rather popular. Most individuals were not reading scholastic materials, or books on psychology and business! Soon, people came to me to ask my opinion on different issues. My mentors saw my growth and gave me a lot of support.

I came to understand that, through studying, opportunities open up. *If I ask the right questions and find the right books, I can get answers to all of my questions*, I realized. I was a magnet for information that would improve my mind, my circumstances and my future.

Just before I was discharged from the Navy, I discovered direct sales and network marketing. I learned about Jim Rohn, Tony Robbins, Zig Ziglar and Les Brown. I continued to read voraciously, I networked, I listened to Black talk radio and attended lectures, workshops and political functions—all in the search for knowledge. I wanted to know *everything*.

Today, I am on my true path and, because of my quest for knowledge, I have the skills and readiness to take advantage of remarkable, once-in-a-lifetime opportunities. And I have come to believe that being resourceful and knowing *where* to go to get the information you need is more empowering than just *knowing* that information. That is key.

Forgive yourself for what you do not know and then set out on your own path to find the answers. Never let lack of knowledge hold you back from your own purpose, your own mission. Never let lack of knowledge define you, or trap you or decide your future.

As is clear from my story, whatever you do over an extended period of time leads to greatness. So start small. Maybe you can't read two or three books a week, but you can find time to read for half an hour a day, an hour, something. When you do small things on a regular basis over a period of time, soon enough you will find that your circumstances have changed dramatically. Start where you are and know that you are getting better every day of your life.

Your awakening could be but a page away.

Haki Ammi is a bestselling author, radio host, entrepreneur, community organizer, speaker, network marketer and a job and career coach. A United States Navy veteran, Haki has served as an EMT/FF for the Baltimore City Fire Department for the past ten years. As a speaker and community organizer, he has collaborated on consciousness-raising and economic empowerment events. Haki majored in business marketing and served as president of SIFE/Students in Free Enterprise. He is currently a part-time representative with Organogold International.

Haki was selected as the community liaison for the newly formed Baltimore Chapter of the Association of Black Psychologists and is an active member of the Association for the Study of Classical African Civilization. He was one of seventy-two people selected from over a thousand contenders to be a part of the Marathon of Excellence, which trains entrepreneurs nationwide. He was also selected to sit on the board of directors as the chair of marketing for the Baltimore Black Chamber of Commerce.

Haki received several awards for military service operations and a community service award for volunteer work from the National Lift Every Voice and Sing Foundation based in Baltimore, Maryland. He is the recipient of the Black Wall Street Award. Haki's work has been featured on Bmorenews.com, and in Baltimore Afro *and* The Baltimore Times. *On radio in Baltimore, he has appeared on* Newsmaker Line for the Larry Young Morning Show *on 1010 AM, and hosted his own show at WFBR 1590 AM. To connect with Haki, visit www.HaramBeeRadio.com and www.SuccessScholarHaki.com.*

DIANE M. LOCKETT

ONE BITE AT A TIME

When I was eighteen, I had my first taste of freedom. I grew up in a two-parent home with a strong Christian foundation. Our family ate dinner together each night at the table. We, kids, had chores and learned respect. There was love and harmony in our home. My parents were strict. So, when I became an adult and the reins came off, I felt free to go to class or just hang out in the student lounge. I could make those decisions on my own for the first time in my life.

Unfortunately, I made some bad decisions. I ended up hanging out in the student lounge a little too often and soon enough I was failing three of my classes. I was headed right for failing out of college entirely. And I was familiar with failure—I saw a lot of it while growing up in the projects.

But one day, God intervened. I was playing basketball in the gym, when I tore three ligaments and some cartilage in my knee. I ended up flat on my back for weeks and had a lot of time to think and to see what was around me. Vacant lots, abandoned buildings, elevators that smelled like urine. My projects weren't even the worst of them—I had a relatively good experience growing up. But there were still teenagers from broken homes on every corner, smoking weed and failing high school. Surely, I did not want to be one of them.

As I lay on my back with nothing else to think of, cast itchy around my leg, I determined that it was my dream to escape, to live somewhere with green grass and a whole and happy home at the end of the day. I wanted to be successful and pave the path that my parents had been unable to tread themselves.

But I had been straying from that ultimate goal. I'd let myself lose my lifelong dream of being a teacher, a professor, someone who could influence the lives of others and motivate them to achieve. I'd started to let my dream slip. And no one cared—no one from the team at school, no one I hung out with cared enough to even call to check on me. I realized then that I had to take charge of my life and rearrange my priorities. I had to do whatever was necessary to get back on course.

I had to do the right thing, because that's how I was raised. And so I started hobbling on crutches as soon as I was able to stand up again. Using a medical excuse, I dropped the classes I was failing and promised myself I would keep up with those I had left. My family only had one car, and cab fare was out of the question. So, I

**It took a lot to make my
ultimate dreams a reality.**

had to take several buses and a train from my home to the campus, regardless of the wind, rain or snow. I carried my duffle bag full of books and somehow managed to limp to class, and I passed. For two and a half years I struggled on crutches or with a cane. It took three years for me to get each degree, but I did it.

I graduated with honors. Up on that stage, getting my diploma, I felt as if I was soaring. My parents were in the crowd. We had plans to go out to dinner—I had achieved something. It felt good to be an achiever. It seemed the worst of the work was behind me. It wasn't, of course, but on that day I was untouchable. I had suffered for three years to get through, and I'd kept the promise I made to myself when I lay flat on my back with an injured knee all those years before. I got the credentials that society requires for success.

I'd put my best foot forward, even if that foot was at the end of an injured leg.

Don't drop your dream! Just as I did, you can overcome the obstacles in your path. The path may be rocky. It may be dark and sinister; but if you keep the light of hope, you can keep on stepping forward.

How do you eat an elephant? One bite at a time. It's important, essential, to prioritize.

Set some goals. Make a to-do list, even if that list is twenty items long. You just have to figure out what the most important thing to do first is, and then work your way down the line, bit by bit, day by

It was not an option to be out of options.

day, goal by goal. And that (with some prayer), can lead you along the way to achieving what you want to achieve. You can make your dreams real that way.

It took a lot to make my ultimate dreams a reality. I didn't magically acquire the grassy home with the whole family I wanted once I'd achieved the first step. I had a lot of struggle to go through, including a terrible marriage and single parenthood. On top of that, I had to go back to school. This, at least, was something I was familiar with. I knew I could make it, if I took it just one step at a time.

I was in my thirties, working as an adjunct professor and raising my two kids on my own when my supervisor at the college advised me to go back to school and get my master's degree. They were changing requirements, and I would soon need a master's degree if I wanted to keep my job. So, I had to go register for classes during a time when I was between paychecks, unable to pay the fees. I tried to make arrangements to defer payments, but I was told that it was no longer an option.

"So what other options do I have?" I asked, and they told me I was out of options. I would have to return the following semester to register when I had the money to do so. But I could not leave that building without registering for classes. My job depended on it. My children depended on me to get it done, because I needed to put food on our table, and I couldn't do that without a job.

It was not an option to be out of options. I was desperate. I left that line and found the office of the head honcho, the man in charge of making the decisions. He was the chief accountant, and I broke down right in front of him. Everything poured out of me, right from my heart, and I remember him offering me tissues to stem my flowing tears.

"Will you help me?" I sobbed as I explained my situation. I was a single mother, abandoned by my husband, who left me with two small children. And I just couldn't take it anymore. I needed to register for classes that semester, or I'd lose my job.

Step-by-step, you can walk your path.

The chief accountant tried to comfort me, saying, "It's going to be all right." He said he'd see what he could do, and he told me to check back with him the next day.

I did just that. At the second meeting, he informed me that the funds were not available through the school, but that he would be willing to make a personal loan to me. Again, I had to check back with him. When I did, I vowed to repay him, to repay his kindness and his faith in a stranger, to repay the risk he'd taken in doing this.

And I did repay him. I burned the candle at both ends and focused on my classes. That's something that people admire, but they don't know the sacrifices I made to get to that point. You hear a lot of no's before you hear a single yes, and then you have to search and plow and stay focused until it comes about.

I stayed focused, and I ate my elephant one bite at a time. I looked in the mirror and saw my children. I saw their next meal, and I made it happen one way or another. I ate mayonnaise sandwiches and beans, or ate nothing at all (my belly grumbling with only water inside it) to make sure my kids had food in their bellies. I went to my classes and earned my master's degree, and I repaid every single dime that chief accountant loaned me.

Today, I am what I sought to become. I'm a motivational speaker and a teacher. It's all because I prioritized, made my lists and crossed the items off that list one-by-one. I have since inspired others to do the same. For example, a friend from back in the day had been laid off from his job for quite some time. One day I asked him, if he could be anything he wanted, what would he be? He said he always wanted to be a doctor, but he felt that it was too late—since he was in his twenties. I encouraged him to pursue his dream, and he asked me to help him with the application process. Years later, he called me with the news that he had become the chief of surgery.

Another friend of mine was enrolled to become a teacher. He would often sit in my classes to observe my teaching techniques. My lifelong friend earned his doctorate degree and is now a school principal. Finally, one of my sisters revealed to me that at the age of fifty-seven, she was motivated to go back and earn her degrees after watching me, her big sister, all these years. That was the most exciting news of all.

You can do it, too. Step-by-step, you can walk your path. You can stay your course, because with God all things are possible; He never gives you a vision without the provisions to carry it out. You just have to stay focused. You may slide a little bit, and you may even slip and fall. Just get back up, brush off the dust and keep on stepping. At the end of the road, you'll find a door of opportunity that will open if you just turn the knob.

Diane M. Lockett is a motivational speaker, award-winning educator, educational consultant, herbalist, literary expert, performing artist and prolific writer with a unique voice that makes words come alive. Professor Lockett is the director of education at Amp Up, LLC., providing transformational leadership seminars for businesses, mentorship programs and youth symposiums. She is committed to helping others overcome adversity to achieve.

A native New Yorker, Professor Lockett graduated with honors from William Howard Taft High School (Bronx, NY) and the City University of New York with majors in economics and business education as well as a minor in English. In her senior year at Herbert H. Lehman College of CUNY, she was nominated for the award of Best Student Teacher of the Year. Professor Lockett has taught on the college level as adjunct lecturer for twenty-two years, in the City University of New York and at Davenport University in Michigan. After relocating to Detroit, Michigan in 1981, she taught business subjects, reading and English congruently in the Detroit Public School system for twenty years.

For many years, Professor Lockett has been dedicated to serving the school system and community by providing inspiration and information. In 1995, she received the Golden Apple Award of Merit for Outstanding Teacher of the Year from Michigan's MetroParent Magazine. In 1999, she was honored "for fifteen years of dedication, loyalty and commitment" at Davenport University (Dearborn, Michigan). She coordinated the 2001 InsideOut Writing Project at Ruddiman Middle School (2000-2001), which led to the publication of Expressions, *a collection of works by Detroit Public School students.*

Professor Lockett is lovingly referred to as "Big Mama" and "The Food Poetess." She was the first poet featured on the website of the Detroit Writers' Guild. Her poem, "Black Man, You Can," won a Distinguished Works Award in their 12th Annual Paul Laurence Dunbar Poetry Contest (1998). Among her published poems, several are featured in Food for the Spirit (A Black History Cookbook) *by the Detroit Black Writers' Guild. In addition, since 1999, a number of businesses have commissioned her poetic expertise and voice for commercials and jingles, which aired over the radio.*

Recognizing the need for multi-cultural diversity in children's literature, Professor Lockett was motivated to write The Adventures of GB (A Gingerbread Boy). *This modern-day tale is an illustration of perseverance by GB, an in-depth character who has feelings, issues and aspirations as he faces the challenges of life and rejection in a world of diversity. It is packaged as a coloring book with a CD and musical soundtrack for children. In addition, GB, comes alive on the pages of a young adult fiction book for teenagers and the young-at-heart.*

Professor Lockett gained acclaim as a dynamic performance artist/ edutainer, who loves to perform for all ages and has creative works for every occasion. She has been featured in venues across the nation, including the 2014 Michigan State Fair, museums, nursing homes, camps, schools, colleges/universities and corporate functions. Her dynamic performance invokes audience participation using interactive tasks and songs that bring characters and culture to life. She remains a force for speaking about her trials and motivating others to focus, believe and achieve. To connect with Professor Lockett, visit www. DianeLockett.com or www.GoAmpUp.com.

LANRE M. LEE

A BETTER MAN

In my late thirties, more than thirty years after he left us, I received a phone call from my father. "I'm in town with my family. I need you to come to the bus station and pick us up."

I was surprised; I didn't know he had planned a trip to visit me. We had reconnected a few months earlier (after I made the decision to find him in order to get answers and find closure). I had traveled out of state to see him and meet my half-siblings, and we engaged in an in-depth conversation.

Then I went back to my life. Though a part of me secretly hoped we'd someday be able to form a father-son relationship, I wasn't sure I'd ever see him again.

Then suddenly, he was on the end of the phone line, waiting for me to come and pick him up. It was an odd request. *Why is he here? Doesn't he have a plan? Why does he need me to pick him up?*

Out of respect, I drove over to the bus station and loaded my father, his wife and my two half-sisters into my car and drove them to a hotel. It was the strangest and most uncomfortable ride of my life. I had three women who were virtual strangers to me in my backseat; my father, whom I barely knew, in the front. Though grown adults just a couple of years younger than me, my sisters whispered like schoolgirls while their mother, the woman for whom my father left my mother, said nothing.

Dying to get out of there, I made myself stay at the hotel for an hour to be polite. As I was getting ready to leave, my father said, "Son, my funds are held up. I need some money, Man."

I looked at him and said, "Wait a minute. You jumped on a Greyhound bus with your family and came all the way to Detroit—*that* was your money!"

"I have to take care of my family," he replied.

His words hit me like a slap in the face. "What did you say?"

"I have to take care of my family," he said again. "I have to make sure they're okay."

In that moment, it dawned on me that he was talking about *his* family, not *our* family. I realized that he never considered me to be family. It was "my daughters" not "your sisters." Worse, he was trying to make it sound as though it was my responsibility to help him take care of his family.

In disbelief, I sat there, trying to wrap my brain around what just happened. *My father never provided any financial support for me or my mother and yet he came all this way, not to see me, but to ask for money so he could take care of his new family!*

I thought back to the difficult years, to the years of poverty, the years of anger, the years of feeling I was to blame for all of it. My father abandoned us when I was a little boy, and I was sure that

His words hit me like a slap in the face.

I had done something wrong, and he hated me for it. Why else would he have left us?

Looking around my father's hotel room, I recalled my mother working two jobs to support me and my sister. I remembered staying at a homeless shelter, the three of us sleeping in a twin-sized bed and all of us cold and hungry; I couldn't wait to get to school so I could eat my first meal. And I recalled my one pair of shoes with holes in the soles. I had cut out a piece of cardboard and placed it inside each shoe to prevent the skin of my feet from touching the ground. Sometimes the entire front of the sole came apart, and I would duct-tape my shoes to keep them from falling apart.

All at once, the feelings of rejection I thought I'd left behind after our last visit came rushing back. Some part of me still wished I had had a father while growing up, someone to provide for us, to guide me, to be my hero. After all of these years, after all I accomplished, I couldn't let go of the old yearning to have a father who would rise to the occasion and take responsibility, to call *me* family, to help *me* in ways only a father could.

Too stunned and overwhelmed to express how I felt, I told my father I would touch base with him the next day. That night, my mind raced with memories and thoughts with which I'd thought I'd long made peace. Successful in my career and happily married

I would be the best father on the face of the planet.

with two young sons, you would think I could let the past stay in the past and let go of any hope for a magical transformation in my father. But the old feelings were back and stronger than ever.

Growing up abandoned by my father, with my mother as head of household, people immediately put me in a negative category. They defined me as someone bound for failure or death because I didn't have anyone to teach me about being a man. I was in the losing category from the moment my father left.

Because my mom worked between three and five jobs, I had no one to help me with my homework or notice when I needed help in a particular area. So I was labeled as learning disabled and "slow." Kids picked on me, called me "dumb" and "retarded." I sounded funny—I was the transplant from New York City. My closest friends had two-parent homes.

Eventually my mother realized I needed her, and she made time to assist me with my studies. With the help of my mother and the father of one of my closest friends, I started to do better, feel better and get better. Throughout high school, I focused on my education.

It was during this time that I began to develop my Seven-Step Plan for Success:

1. Surround yourself with positive people.
2. Identify life's choices.
3. Develop strategies for a plan of action to achieve.
4. Identify people who provide positive guidance, such as ministers, teachers, coaches, parents and other family members.
5. Through perseverance, begin to implement your selected goals.
6. Stay on target: maintain a positive attitude, have faith, take inventory and shift gears when necessary to accommodate change.
7. For encouragement, maintain an open line of communication with those who have demonstrated a sincere desire to help you achieve.

Following my Seven-Step Plan for Success, I went on to receive numerous accolades for academics, leadership and several scholarships in athletics. I was a Rosa Parks Scholar and a recipient of the McDonald's Black History Maker of Tomorrow Award. But there was always a void, a hole in my heart made by my father's absence.

When my short-lived playboy ways resulted in becoming a dad at nineteen, I was determined to break the cycle. I would support my son, spend time with my son, raise my son; I would be the father I longed for while growing up. Unfortunately, due to custody issues, I wasn't able to spend as much time with Tarik as I planned to. I provided for him financially, but I was only permitted to see him on a limited basis. It ate me up inside, thinking my son could be feeling alone, or unwanted because of the situation.

Sitting at my kitchen table now, I thought back to the devastating Good Friday in 2009 when I received a phone call from my oldest sister.

She'd said, "Get over here right now," but didn't want to tell me why.

Finally, she told my wife, who came to me with tears in her eyes and said, "Tarik killed himself."

Shaking, I fell to my knees. I was in shock, not really believing what they were telling me. It was as if I thought he had attempted suicide, but had not been successful. I kept saying, "Where is he? Tell me where Tarik is!"

When it had finally sunk in that Tarik was gone, the world went still. I had lost my firstborn, my hope, my boy. I didn't know whom to blame. A month after his passing, my stepfather died, and the weight of grief was too much. I went into a state of solitude and shut down from the world. It was a difficult time for me and everyone around me, and I wasn't sure how to come back to myself. I did not know how to mourn.

I fell back on the founding principles my mother taught me: God, family and education. I was told never to question God, but to ask God a question. So I asked, "God, how can I pull myself up from this dark place?" It was from that moment forward that I began to realize I couldn't change the past. There was nothing I could do, no way I could change the outcome of yesterday. *I'm in control of today*, I thought, *and I'm in control of impacting tomorrow.*

Right then and there I made up my mind that I would be the best father on the face of the planet. I would be the best provider I could be; I would saturate myself in the love of my family and in faith. *I will sacrifice myself totally and become selfless; I will become the proper man I was destined to be.* Finally, when I had enough strength to rise, I got up. I applied my Seven-Step Plan for Success to my mission and forged ahead.

Remembering that fateful day now, all I could think about was how many hopes I had pinned on reuniting with my father. Suddenly it was clear why the shock of his request—*I need money to take care of my family*—was so disturbing. It wasn't just that I had grown up with nothing because of his selfish choices. It wasn't just that my mother exhausted herself to support us. It wasn't just that I didn't have a man to help shape me, nurture me and lead by example. It was because I had thought establishing a relationship with him would be my opportunity for redemption, as if he could somehow help me heal the wounds of Tarik's death—one father to another. And yet here I was, contemplating giving my father money to support the only family that mattered to him. There was no sign of the hero I once imagined and still hoped would show up.

The next day, I picked up some breakfast for my father and his family and drove to meet him at the hotel. I wanted to make sure they were okay, that they had enough to eat. As I looked over at the takeout bags on the front seat, I remembered the three things he gave me: a Bible, a gold ring engraved with my initials and a pair of sneaker skates with blue and gold stripes. That's it; that's all he ever gave me.

When I dropped off the food, I explained to my father that it wouldn't be right for me to give him money. In the months that followed, he called me several more times asking for money. There was no need to respond.

My feelings were crushed, but the experience helped me close a chapter in my life. As disappointing as it was, I no longer felt my father could fix me, heal me or make anything right. I no longer wondered if my life would have been better if I had grown up with him—clearly, it would have been worse. And I no longer had the question, "What if?" I felt that God had answered my lifelong question, "Please, may I see my father and get closure." It was as if God said, "Here it is, son. See for yourself."

I'm a better man because of that experience. I learned the true value of stretching outside my comfort zone. I learned that by facing the uncomfortable truth about my father, I was able to get outside of myself and grow and develop. I was able to let go of the imaginary hero I carried around with me for so long, and I became my *own* superhero.

In sports, stretching is part of your warm-up routine. It can be painful stretching all of your muscles; you feel the pull and the burn. But when you stretch, an amazing thing happens: Your blood cells are revived. You gain energy you didn't know you had, and over time, you become more flexible and less prone to injury. The more you stretch, the better you feel and the better you perform.

In life, stretching outside of your comfort zone, facing the truth about your past and letting it go is the key to becoming your own superhero and to becoming successful. Ultimately, the only way I could really stretch, breathe and release was to write a poem about my father. It was my way of finally letting go.

I haven't forgotten my father's choices and the impact they had on our lives, but I understand. I no longer harbor feelings I had since I was a child. I've let the animosity go. I see now that my mother's struggle, all my father did not do to care for us and raise us, is what made me the man I am today—a better man. I would not for one moment want to be away from my sons. I love them. I couldn't imagine being without them. I will teach them to be responsible, educated men, good citizens who contribute to society—not because I didn't have a father while growing up, but because I had such an exceptional mother. With God's help, my sons will be fine.

Sometimes, life just isn't fair. Sometimes the people we need the most seem to be without feeling, cold-hearted and callous. But with God, all things are possible. The newness of life is seen in the way we triumph over adversity. Despite the odds, despite the stereotypes, despite the racial inequities and social injustices, you can be successful.

The station you are in right now, the place where you're standing, or lying down—does not define you. The ultimate test of who you are is the way you rise and work through your challenges and circumstances. Yes, you may work at McDonald's right now. Yes, you may have a junky car. Yes, you may not have two parents. But this does not determine your success in the future. You are the master of your fate, the captain of your soul. Let no one define you. You are superhuman. You will grow and stretch and maximize your potential—but it's on you to get it done.

"Small" Talk (Part 1)
by Lanre M. Lee

See, I've been waiting a really long time
To tell you what's been on my mind.

I was born without a choice in the matter
Somehow, I had no voice in the chatter

But I'm here. So, I'll vent how I'm concerned
In hopes you understand how respect is earned.

You and Mom loved, married and had us.
Then you, two, broke up due to things adulterous.

Now, what does that mean? Just us...it was tough!
Mom, Big Sis and me! Yeah, we had it rough!

Mom never said much but, "Dad's on his way."
You never came by or called for 2-5 days.

The days turned to weeks, weeks to months, and we had to leave.
So, Mom packed us up and moved us to the "D"!

I hated Detroit! An outcast with an accent,
How could I fit in? My culture was different.

The real question was, "Would I ever blend in?"
I was so different, how could I find a friend?

I was used to trains, cabs and the bus
Not fancy cars, no family, just us!

To a young boy, tell me, how do you cope
In the land of Young Boyz Incorporated...City of Dope?

Grandpapa would call and send for us
Back in New York by plane, train or bus.

I would brag, "I'mma see my Dad, my cousins and stuff."
We stayed for months, no call, no show, no luck.

Mom finally found you, and your new woman's lies.
She said, "He's not here!" when she looked in my eyes.

My mom threw a fit. Then you came out
Big Sis and I watching our Mom and Dad shout.

I remember you saying you'll send money and visit.
You never came…got word you're living exquisite.

As for us, Dad, we stayed in a shelter, 3 in a twin bed
I still remember like yesterday, falling and bumping my head.

In the middle of the night, I went quickly back to sleep.
Praying that the hunger pangs would stop torturing me deep.

Many nights were cold. We didn't know when we would eat.
Detroit had harsh winters. We had no coats or boots on our feet.

Mom never complained. She worked two and three jobs.
An educated woman, but it was still hard.

God provided. We got a house and a car.
We were close to living nice, but still very far.

Then the bombshell hit. My Papa had died.
Still no call from you, Dad. How much I cried.

I saw life as cruel and unusually hard.
Mom gave hugs and kisses, then said, "Be faithful to God!"

My Big Sis got pregnant at a very young age,
And the father of her baby was much older, past her stage.

My nephew grew up in my house like my little brother.
Mom worked like Mom and Dad, Big Sis was a sister and mother.

As confusing as that sounds, it painted a vivid picture in my mind
With all this anger inside, I'm hoping I would find
A way I could live,
Escape this and live more positive

Maybe I could close my eyes and on the chalkboard inside my eyelids
Somehow I could erase life...rewrite the story to sound more positive...

I searched every Holy scripture for the answer (Give that a thought)
Only to return to the beginning of what I was taught.

What I sought was peace! The peace of knowing I despised you.
Dad, you abandoned your family to start one anew!

If you, two, could not get along, I could understand.
Leaving your children? How do I measure a man?

Just so you know, I refused to be a punk, so I hit the street.
Got my education, hustled to make ends meet.

By God's Grace, my friends' mom and dad helped raise me.
You didn't care enough to see what kind of son I would be.
Thirty years later, you popped back up with ease.
Just for a minute. Gone like a summer breeze.

Even through all of these hardships, God had a master plan.
Dad, I forgive you. 'Cause I'm a better man.

—By: Lanre M. Lee, 1/2013

Lanre M. Lee is the founder and president of Amp Up Leadership Institute, a consultation organization focused on engaging leadership through an educational lens. A division of AMP UP, LLC, Amp Up Leadership Institute is a curriculum-based program directed to motivate and inspire through transformational leadership seminars for business, mentorship programs and youth symposiums.

Lanre graduated from the University of Michigan, where he received the Distinguished Student Leadership Award and was recognized for his research in gang violence in the public school system. He is a published researcher for the Harvard Pluralism Project under the direction of Dr. Claude Jacobs. He has served on many boards concerning at-risk youth. Lanre was also elected as the first African-American Director of Clubs and Organizations at the University of Michigan, and was elected president of the Association of African-American students.

Upon entering corporate America, Lanre was quickly recognized as a top-producing manager and business leader. Despite many obstacles, he persevered as an achiever and earned a number of prestigious awards, including the McDonald's Black History Maker of Tomorrow Award and the Detroit Rotary Club Citizen of the Month Award.

Lanre was awarded the Rosa Parks Scholarship, presented by Mother Rosa Parks, herself, and the Rosa Parks Scholarship Foundation. He appeared in many public service announcements promoting the Rev. Dr. Martin Luther King Service Day. On February 4, 2013, the National Rosa Parks' Day of Courage, Lanre M. Lee received recognition on the Public Broadcasting Service (PBS). On a later date, he was selected by Delora Tyler, former president of the Rosa Parks Scholarship Foundation, to represent the foundation as a successful award recipient. During the interview on TV-CW 50, he reflected on the impact that the scholarship had on his life and he explained his Seven-Step Plan for Success (which he still applies effectively today).

Lanre received handwritten letters from The White House and the Pentagon and was selected to work on healthcare reform with Vice President Al Gore and Congressman John Dingell. In 2013, Lanre received a personal invitation and attended President Barack Obama's *inauguration, as well as the Close-Up Foundation's Congressional reception.*

Lanre is an active member of the Omega Psi Phi Fraternity, Inc. (Nu Omega Chapter). Mr. Lee is happily married with children. He is constantly in the pursuit of excellence and academia while striving to motivate others to achieve despite the odds. He is available for speaking engagements and seminars globally. Connect with Lanre at www.GoAmpUp.com.

RUSS BARNES

THE DREAM ROUTINE

When I open my front door, the early morning air is cool and clean. The sky is dark, with countless stars overhead. I am alone—not a person or car is in sight. From the moment my feet hit the pavement for the first step of what will be a five-mile circuit around the golf course, I am committed to this run.

Today, I will run five miles—just as I did yesterday, and the day before. And tomorrow, I will get up and do it again. I will run five miles, every morning, before sunrise. Rain or shine, no matter how late I stayed up the night before, regardless of my mood, I will get it done. I have a goal, and this is my routine to make it happen.

In 2009, I set a goal to run a half-marathon in under two hours. While on military assignment in Saudi Arabia, I joined a group of runners training for a half-marathon. When I saw that I finished the race in two hours and two minutes, I said, "I know I can finish in under two hours."

Stationed in Tampa, Florida the following year, I approached my goal the same way I have done since college—I broke it down. I thought, "I want to run thirteen and one-half miles in under two hours. What do I need to do to get there?" I figured out that I would have to run at least five miles every day, in forty-five minutes or less, to be prepared to reach my goal. Running in the morning before work was my best option for two reasons: By nine o'clock it was brutally hot, and the morning was the only time of day when I was positive that nothing would interrupt my routine.

In order to accomplish my daily morning runs with my schedule, which required that I leave the house by five-fifteen a.m. to be at my desk by six, I realized that I would have to get up at three forty-five in the morning in order to be on the road by four. This may be where I lose you. For most people, getting up before six seems impossible, let alone before four! I used to believe that myself, until I made my decision.

When the appointed time arrived, I did not question the wisdom *or* the decision—it was no longer up for debate. Day after day, I simply executed the routine. I didn't think "I'm tired" or "I have a long day today." I just got up and did it. And I did it, and I did it, and I did it.

By following my routine, I was able to achieve my goal. My predawn, five-mile daily run was the routine that enabled me to finish the 2010 Gasparilla Half-Marathon in one hour and fifty-four minutes!

Merriam-Webster defines routine as "a regular course of procedure." No one runs a mile, much less a half-marathon, with a single step. You cannot build a house with a single brick; a baby

I would have to get up at three forty-five in the morning in order to be on the road by four.

is not ready for birth after a single month. Achievement is a steady progress using a proven process—*a regular course of procedure*—and if you can make your effort part of a routine, you will have essentially put success on automatic.

On game days, Miami Heat's famed shooter Ray Allen shows up to the arena three and one-half hours before tipoff to practice shooting. Good day or bad day, he works the same intense twenty-minute routine he's followed for more than fifteen years, since his second season in the NBA.

"Everyday Ray," as his coaches and teammates refer to him, is still living his dream at thirty-four, an age when most professional basketball players are retired or on their way out. One of the best shooters of all time with an NBA-record 3,344 three-pointers made in his career, Allen's routine is legend. People come to the arena early just to watch him practice, and so many of his teammates have joined him in his daily efforts that the team bus is required to transport them all to the arena.

Allen attributes his long-term success to his routine, which is more than just the twenty minutes of concentrated shooting. His entire lifestyle is geared toward his goal of successfully delivering points in every game. Nutrition, exercise, practice, down time— every choice he makes is geared toward that one goal.

The stronger your motivation, the more discipline you'll have.

Routine achieves results, but it's you who decides which results you achieve. The fact is, routine has always played a role in your life. Until now, however, your routine may not have been focused on helping yourself.

What is your favorite television show? What time does it air? How often do you miss it? Watching it is a routine. And what was the tradeoff for that routine? What *didn't* you do so as not to miss your show? And there it is: the results, or lack thereof. This is the kind of routine we seldom admit we follow or may even want to give up. But we also have other routines that we are not always aware of, daily practices that garner positive results.

For example, my wife and I read books to our sons every night when we put them to bed. This practice fostered togetherness and a love of reading in our kids, and stimulated their imagination. You may read to your children every day, or pray every morning. You may call your mom every Saturday, or write in a journal. All of these routine practices have positive, long-range payoffs.

While these simple routines may seem reasonable to you, you may have read my story about getting up every day at three forty-five to train for the half-marathon, or Ray Allen's story about practicing before games, and thought, "There's no way I could do that. You must be crazy." This is not where I tell you that you're wrong. Of course you wouldn't do what I did. You wouldn't do it because you don't want what I wanted. The key to achieving any goal—and I do mean *any* goal, no matter how "crazy"—is, you have to want it badly enough. When what you want is important enough to you, you will establish—and stick with—a routine to achieve the results you desire.

When my children were young, they played on a basketball team. After listening to some of the other parents talking at games and practices, my wife asked me, "Why don't you push the boys to shoot two hundred baskets a day, like the other dads?"

"Games should be fun," I replied. "When the boys *want* to shoot baskets, I'm happy to do it."

As they developed a love for the game—because they were having fun—they eventually started going outside after school every day to shoot *more* than two hundred baskets. They did more than the other kids on their team because they *wanted* to play better, not because they were forced to do so. They accomplished more through internal motivation than they ever would have if they were simply being driven to do it.

Motivation activates discipline. The stronger your motivation, the more discipline you'll have available to achieve the goal. Anything you want to achieve can be achieved if your internal motivation is sufficient. Then, the path is clear: Break it down into routine, manageable steps. It really is that simple. This is how I earned several degrees while serving in the military and raising four children. This is how I ran the half-marathon in under two hours. This is how I read the entire Bible in ninety days. This is how I learned German. This is how I saved enough money to buy my own franchise territory upon retirement from the military.

If your internal motivation is solid but you still find you're procrastinating taking action with your goal, it may be that there is too much distance between where you are and where you want to go. During aviation training early in my military career, I went through survival training, often in forests. We were each given a compass for land navigation and a designated point and told: "Pick a heading that will get you where you want to go."

When you walk in a forest, you can't move in a straight line. There are trees in the way, and ponds and rivers. The only way to get to your destination is to pick a heading to a target, such as a tree, and then go to that tree. When you get there you pick another tree, or boulder, or other distinctive target, and walk toward it.

**Once you establish your routine,
you won't want to break it.**

We all know the saying, "You can't see the forest for the trees." Well, this is how you use the trees to get through the forest. In other words, by focusing on the small steps—the trees—you are able to achieve your goal one step at a time.

When you apply my "Routine Achieves Results" method, no dream is impossible, no goal too big. Even the most overwhelming and terrifying mission can be completed when you break down your goal and create a strategy that involves a daily routine you can execute within the confines of your life and work commitments.

Once you establish your routine, you won't want to break it. You'll get up at the crack of dawn every day to write half a page of your book, even if you feel blocked. You'll show up to the gym to work out, even if you're tired. You'll put money aside every month, even if you'd rather spend it on something else. You'll make time to study, and practice, and read and meditate—whatever your dream requires, you will follow the routine to the letter.

Colonel (Ret.) Russell C. Barnes is a decorated military officer, speaker and author. An expert on the fundamentals of vision, mission and core values, Colonel Barnes draws from his twenty-seven years in the military to help people master the disciplinary excellence required to achieve even the most far-reaching goals. When assigned as Chief of the J5 Policy Division, Headquarters, USCENTCOM, Tampa, Florida, Colonel Barnes developed his "Routine Achieves Results" goal-achievement method, which he now uses to assist veterans in their transition to civilian careers.

A graduate of United States Air Force Weapons School, Bomber Division, Colonel Barnes holds a bachelor's degree in computer information systems from Manhattan College and a master's degree in business administration with an emphasis on aviation from Embry-Riddle University. He completed Squadron Officer School, Air Command and Staff College, Armed Forces Staff College and Air War College, and was awarded a second master's degree in strategic studies from Air University, Air War College, where he won the Red River Valley Award for Best Strategy Paper in 2003.

Colonel Barnes is a Master Navigator with over three thousand hours in T-37, T-43, B-52G and B-52H aircraft. His military awards and decorations include the Legion of Merit, Air Medal, Defense Meritorious Service Medal, Meritorious Service Medal with oak leaf cluster, Air Force Commendation Medal with oak leaf cluster, Joint Service Achievement Medal, Air Force Outstanding Unit Award with Valor Device and two oak leaf clusters, Combat Readiness Medal with two oak leaf clusters, National Defense Service Medal, Southwest Asia Service Medal, Kuwaiti Liberation Medals for Kuwait and Saudi Arabia, Expert Marksmanship Ribbon and Air Force Unit Excellence Award. He was promoted to Colonel on September 1, 2005 and retired from the Air Force on December 1, 2009.

To connect with Colonel Barnes, visit www.linkedin.com/in/ RCBarnes.

JAMES J. WILLIAMS

I PLEDGE ALLEGIANCE TO MY DREAMS

It was a Monday morning when I returned to work after a relaxing and spirit-filled weekend away with my wife. I was ready to attack any obstacles coming my way and I walked into the office with a smile.

Before I could even hang up my jacket, however, I was asked to see the manager. Unbeknownst to me, I'd initially been hired under a ninety-day contract. They had never shared with me that the contract was already as good as over, just that they needed someone to come in and assist with streamlining the process of their own contract renewals—and I had never asked.

Now, I had to turn in my badge and leave the building immediately. I was calm and relaxed. As my colleagues watched me collect up my belongings, I told them, "Guys, it really has been a pleasure, and I appreciate the opportunity."

Their faces were telling to say the least; I suspect they anticipated fireworks from me. I shook the hands of both my immediate supervisor and the program manager and exchanged pleasantries with the security guard as I made my exit, never to return. Every step I took toward my car made my brain feel heavier, and it was as if I opened the car door while standing on my head.

All at once, it occurred to me exactly what had just happened: I had been let go. How was I going to break the news to my wife?

We had been married only six months and were living out of boxes in a one-bedroom apartment while our new home was under construction. It was due to be completed in a matter of months, and our son was due to be born around the same time. *What am I going to do?* I thought as I drove home.

Only through years of practice was I able to keep myself from total panic. I grew up the eldest of four children in a single-parent family in Cleveland, Ohio. My father had walked away from us when the responsibility got too much, and so it naturally fell to me to assume the role not only of eldest child and older brother, but father figure as well.

When I was six years old, my brother and I watched our mother going to the county welfare office because she couldn't make ends meet, and I did not want that to be my life again. It couldn't be my life, not after everything I had achieved.

Living in the inner city, it never really seemed possible to dream or to want more for myself than what I'd been given. Because of my family's economic status, almost everyone around me—including

I had to turn in my badge and leave the building immediately.

my high school guidance counselor—seemed to think that higher education was out of reach. But I knew that getting my high school diploma and going on to work a regular nine-to-five job would never be the kind of fulfillment I was seeking, so the only thing that made sense was to work harder and keep chasing the dream that I knew was there waiting to be achieved.

During my sophomore year, I was accepted into the highly competitive Upward Bound program, which exposed me and the other participants' to a wide variety of cultural, educational and social experiences.

That proved to be a stepping stone into gaining the scholarship I needed to access the higher education toward which I'd been working for years. It was the first domino to fall in a long line of opportunities that would lead me to the Army Reserves in 1988, proudly and honorably serving my nation while also attending college courses.

By 2004 and that fateful day of walking back out of the office less than thirty minutes after walking in, I had served in many operations—not least of which was Operation Iraqi Freedom. *Corporate America didn't really care about the military veterans— they cared about keeping the money turning over,* I thought. My grip was tight on the steering wheel as I drove home; I felt bitter and betrayed by everyone and everything.

My early childhood experiences had made me feel inadequate, as if I couldn't compete in the workforce. It took me more than a decade to get my bachelor's degree due to circumstances beyond my control, and I was woefully unprepared to be as competitive as my Ivy League counterparts. I felt that my employers had

I'd failed to ask the questions.

conspired against me and were determined to deny my potential and limit opportunity; even the knowledge that I had just served a two-year military assignment and was recently married with a child on the way did nothing to sway my employer's decision to show me the door.

My wife, Greta, was waiting for me by the door when I entered our cluttered apartment. Without procrastinating, because there really was no way around it, I shared what had happened at the office.

I began, "This is not what I had in mind for our life together."

As I spoke, I became deeply bitter about what had just occurred, but I chose not to display it as she did not need added stress while pregnant. Now I did not have health coverage for my wife or our unborn child. Thankfully, through her employer—she did! Nonetheless, this challenged my manhood in ways I cannot articulate. Being at the mercy of an outside institution other than the military to care for my family and me was a foreign concept.

I said, "We just experienced a spirit-filled worship experience. There has to be a lesson to all of this, but I'm not sure what that lesson is."

Although Greta was quiet, her eyes said it all: James, I believe in you, but I'm a little scared.

Wow! I'm six months into my first marriage. I'm close to forty years old, and I cannot offer my unborn child my own history. I'd barely had time to shake off what had happened during my term of service before I was getting married, trying to set up house and expecting my first child. It was too soon to have all of these difficulties at once, but I couldn't let my own past become my child's future.

You didn't wait until forty to marry and have children to let them have the same start in life you did, I thought, carefully considering my next move.

The first thing I did was to think about where I had gone wrong. From a young age I had developed a practice of putting everything down on paper: shortcomings and dreams and steps I needed to take to achieve both success and freedom, two fundamental building blocks toward fulfillment.

I knew that my work was consistently of a high caliber, and so my being let go couldn't have been as a result of neglecting my duties. I'd failed to ask the right questions: the information about the length of contract hadn't been volunteered, this much was true, but neither had I asked.

I wasn't content with labeling myself as a victim—and moreover, I didn't have time to be a victim! I'd never been one, not even when I was ten years old and Christmas had had to be "canceled" because we had no money, and I'd sat with my brothers and sisters in tears around a bare Christmas tree.

Even though I had lost this particular battle, I was still a victor. Now when I started applying for jobs, I was a little picky; I had a very good skillset and didn't want a job just for job's sake. I was an assertive college graduate, a husband and a soon-to-be father with a dream to fulfill and no time to waste.

80

At interviews, this time I asked the questions: "How long is the contract? What happens if a contract terminates early? Do you provide reserve systems for employees between one contract ending and the next beginning?"

All the while, I was putting things down on paper: What I wanted to achieve; how to go about achieving it; and how to turn those achievements into my ultimate, fulfilling goal of success plus freedom. It was going to be on my own terms, and I wasn't going to let the thief in my mind steal my promise—I didn't allow other people to do it, so why would I do it to myself?

For most individuals, the thief in their minds stops them from pursuing their promise, but so can people around them. Oftentimes, you find yourself at the mercy of someone else's guidance, and this

Write your success plan down on paper.

may be the wrong kind of guidance, because they don't see you as you see yourself.

After losing that job, it only took a matter of weeks for me to exceed not only my own expectations, but the expectations of those who doubted my abilities in the first place. By 2013, I was serving as an Army Chief Warrant Officer to the United States Pacific Command in Camp Smith, Hawaii; my initial two-year assignment had even been extended by a year, with the possibility of a permanent posting there.

There's a joke that goes, "If you have nine broke friends, you'll be number ten." You have to align yourself with people who are either doing what you're doing or are on their way to it. Go to people who are pursuing their dreams, those who can give you the "Aha!" moments and jump-start your thinking, and this thinking should begin with: I have the capacity to *decide,* to not be the thief of my own dreams, to write down what I want to achieve and match it with effort.

I urge you to pledge who *you* want to be, not what someone else believes you should be. My good mentor, George C. Fraser, often says that if you don't build your dream, someone else will hire you to build theirs. Even if you do have to focus on other work in the short term, never lose sight of your personal dream. Your dream may lay dormant or in hibernation until due season. Once your season awakens you, it is time to act on it. My dream of owning and operating my own business was always in the forefront of my mind. I was not ready for that either financially or in maturity. I pursued dream jobs that became stepping stones for me until I was fired from my job. With that, my entrepreneurial flame immediately ignited.

I encourage you to write your success plan down on paper. It really works. I have milestones and objectives that date as far back as January 2000. Then, ask the right questions. Do not skirt around what you are inquiring about in making your final decision, whether it is a job, purchasing a home, attending or returning to school for a degree. Ask! My failure did not come from being fired, but because I did not ask the right question about the expiration date of the current contract. Had I known that it was only ninety days, I would have made a different decision.

Don't expect allegiance to be pledged to you just because you have pledged allegiance to others. What kinds of success, freedom and fulfillment could you achieve if you dedicated your energies to pledging allegiance to your own dreams instead?

James J. Williams is an author, consultant, speaker, veteran, adjunct instructor and entrepreneur. He is the founder of Rising Eagle Publishing LLC., an independent veteran-owned publishing company chartered to provide consulting and publishing services to indie and unknown authors. He is also the author of the award-winning book Chasing the Eagle: From Dreaming to Achieving Success and Freedom. *His career spans more than twenty-five years as an information technology and human resources professional in both the government sector and private industry, and he is currently serving his more than twenty-five-year career as Chief Warrant Officer in the United States Army Reserves. To learn more about how you can pledge allegiance to your dreams, connect with James at www.JamesJosephWilliams.com. For interest in his book, visit www.ChasingTheEagle.com, and for publishing services visit www.RisingEaglePublishing.com.*

LYNNETTE ROGERS

STEP OUT OF YOUR COMFORT ZONE

"Does anyone have any questions?"

Five words that, for most of my life filled me with dread. For as long as I can remember, I had a terrible fear of speaking in public. I had ideas, thoughts and opinions that I wanted to share but I allowed this terror to mute me.

When I was in class or attending a meeting or seminar, and the speaker would ask, "Does anyone have any questions?" or, "Would anyone like to offer any feedback?" I would freeze up. Although I wanted to leap up out of my seat and share, I would remain silent, paralyzed, only to hear someone else say the same thing I was thinking or wanted to say, or would leave with the questions I had unanswered. This experience happened to me many times, and I became used to the idea that my thoughts were okay inside my head. *What I have to say isn't important anyway,* I thought.

I grew up the middle child. For many years I had dreamt of being a news broadcaster or a talk-show host, or working in some area where I was facilitating lively discussions around important issues. I remember a time when I was a freshman in high school when I had an opportunity to join the broadcasting team. The broadcasting team had the chance to learn all about news broadcasting and journalism and made the school's daily announcements live.

I was excited and wanted to take advantage of this opportunity, so I made arrangements to stay after school to try out. I visualized myself as the *best* broadcaster in the world and began practicing some of the material we were given for the tryouts.

When the day came, that feeling of doubt crept over me when I saw other students waiting to go in. The voice inside my head started speaking to me, saying things like, "You're not as good as them," and, "You're not going to make it" and, "Everyone is going to make fun of you." I felt very self-conscious and my enthusiasm disappeared.

When it was my turn, I had to sit behind the makeshift broadcasting table and read the announcements. The area was set up just like a news broadcasting room with the camera operator, audiovisual equipment and producer. When they gave me the cue to begin, I froze like a deer in headlights, and the words just couldn't come out. When I did manage to say a few words, I was speaking low, looking down at my script reading it word for word and making no connection with the "audience." Everyone

When they gave me the cue to begin, I froze.

else who was auditioning was watching, and I could hear them laughing and whispering to each other, making fun of me. I was embarrassed and told the producer, "I can't do it." I gave up and ran out. I felt horrible and decided that I needed to explore other options as a career choice because broadcasting and speaking was not for me!

After I graduated from high school and began my first year in college, I chose communications as my major. I still had a burning desire to be a better communicator and pursue my dream in the area of broadcasting and journalism. But as opportunities presented themselves for me to go farther down that path, I allowed self-doubt and negative self-talk to persuade me to change my major to something I thought was more "low-key" and out of the limelight: business administration.

I was able to get jobs as an administrative assistant at some great companies where I gained a lot of experience and eventually found myself nestled in my comfort zone, working a nine-to-five in a cubicle safely under the radar at General Motors (GM) headquarters in downtown Detroit. Although my dreams were still alive and inside of me, nudging, tugging on me, I continued to ignore my dreams and stayed in my comfort zone.

In November 2009, I got the dreaded tap on the shoulder and was informed that, due to the economic downturn and what was happening in the auto industry, my job assignment was ending. As a single mother of three children, I didn't know what I was going

I was determined to overcome this fear.

to do. As that old saying goes, "When it rains, it pours." Well, after I lost my job, my grandmother, with whom I was very close, fell ill, had a stroke and soon passed away. Not long after that I lost my car and my home!

I felt alone, afraid and broken. My children were very young and, although my job at GM had afforded me a comfortable lifestyle, I had spent many hours away from them working and they had become "latch-key" kids. I had to change my circumstances, but I didn't want another "job" for which my time and talents were leveraged by someone else.

I received a call from a longtime friend who shared with me a business opportunity. It was a way for me to earn an income in the comfort of my own home.

I told him, "As long as I don't have to get in front of people, I'm on board."

I didn't want to do any sales. He assured me that he would be right by my side to assist me in building my new business and not to worry about anything else. As I continued building my new business, I became totally dependent on my friend and business partner to do all of our presentations. Our business began to grow and everything was going fine until I'd want to plan events, or ask him to present. Because of his hectic travel schedule, he was often unavailable.

He'd say, "Lynnette, you can do the presentation, you know this business inside-out. It's time for you to do it."

He was right. I *did* know everything about the business and our products and services and could probably have given an amazing presentation, but I refused to step outside of my comfort zone. As time went on, my business partner crisscrossed the country building the business, and I was afraid to open my mouth to talk to people, becoming increasingly frustrated.

I had also begun another business from home, but because I wasn't comfortable selling and promoting my services, I began to struggle financially.

I had to do something quick or go find a job, which I did not want to do. I enjoyed my time freedom and being available to my children. I made the commitment to do something about my fear of speaking. I was determined to overcome this fear that I had allowed to cripple me for far too long.

I found a quote I heard once to be very true, "Nothing is more powerful than a made-up MIND!" My mind was made up, and I set off on a journey of personal development and self-improvement. I joined a Toastmasters club to help me overcome my fear of public speaking, changed my circle of friends, nurtured my dreams and set goals for myself regularly. I shifted my mindset by eliminating negative self-talk and replacing it with positive self-talk and positive energy.

The first time I stood up in front of my Toastmasters club to introduce myself, my heart was beating out of my chest. But everyone was so friendly and encouraging—soon I was standing up to speak at every meeting.

It was a slow process that required me to face my fears every day. In Toastmasters we are encouraged to look for opportunities to practice in everyday life. After a lifetime of shrinking whenever asked, "Does anyone have a question?" I would have to summon the courage to speak up.

As one of my daily challenges, I'd call random talk radio stations to make comments. I figured, "Nobody knows me; no one will recognize my voice." I was just a random person on the radio, no reason to freeze up. It was a safe way to begin breaking out of my comfort zone. I used my middle name—Michelle—and finally opened my mouth to be heard.

Every day, after I dropped my kids off at school, I called in to a radio show. And every day, it got easier. On one call, the host was so impressed by what I shared about my journey as an entrepreneur

I discovered a whole new side of me.

she asked to interview me during the entrepreneur segment of her talk show. I had to fess up. "My first name is actually Lynnette." The producer laughed when she heard my reasons. And that was it—Lynnette was out front.

After that interview my business took off. I received so many calls from individuals wanting my services. I became fully committed to seeing my mission through to the end and dedicating myself to continuing my journey of self-improvement and personal development and to helping others on their journey as well. I still call talk radio shows to continue to challenge myself!

One of my turning points came when I gave a speech at my Toastmasters club, and a gentleman approached me and said, "I was so moved and motivated by your words, I had to know more about you. Could you possibly help me overcome my fear of speaking in public and become a better communicator?"

He became my first coaching client, and I realized I wanted to help others who feared public speaking or wanted to improve their public speaking skills.

My life has changed in some amazing ways since I decided to challenge myself and stepped outside of my comfort zone. I'm a public speaker and public speaking trainer and coach. I've won Toastmasters club competitions; I belong to three clubs and have served as president of the first club I joined! My businesses are still running successfully and growing, and I also started a non-profit organization where I mentor youth in the area of public speaking, communication and leadership.

Engaging in this process and working on myself, I discovered a whole new side of me I had no idea was there. All I wanted to do was get over the fear of speaking so I could get better results in my business. Everything shifted and took on a whole new life of its own. Even now, people tell me, "There's no way you were afraid to talk."

It's a beautiful thing—I had made a huge mountain out of my fear and it hindered me for *so* many years. Today, I make myself as open, authentic and relatable as possible, and doors to amazing experiences, opportunities and results open with ease.

Successful people are no different from you. We all face obstacles, challenges and hardships at some point in our lives. If I can overcome the many challenges, hardships and obstacles I've faced in my life, you can too! Even if you've been avoiding something you've feared for most of your life, you don't have to accept that as your reality.

Make up your mind and then take the first step out of your comfort zone. Stay committed to your personal growth and development and be patient with the process of change that takes place on the journey. Get ready for amazing results!

Lynnette Rogers is a mom and owner of the virtual assistant firm Virtually Yours. She was born in Kileen, Texas but was raised in Detroit, Michigan. After attending Clark Atlanta University, Lynnette came back to Detroit to pursue a career in the automotive industry and later became an entrepreneur. She is the author of The Power of the Made-Up Mind *and* Your Blindspots—Top Reasons You're Not Achieving Your Dreams and Goals. *Connect with Lynnette at www. LynnetteRogers.com.*

DELARIUS MADDEN

NEVER SETTLE—SURPASS!

I stood on the threshold of a foreclosed home I was planning to purchase as an investment with my heart beating wildly, excited by this new venture I wanted to undertake. I walked through the living room, through each of the three bedrooms, the kitchen and the bathroom. Instead of seeing the dilapidated wreck that it currently was, I let my imagination repair the flooring, lay new carpeting and patch the damaged walls. I could visualize fresh paint, new ceilings, a shining kitchen and a sturdy roof.

Each door in that house led me to dream of a new life for each of those rooms. They had me hoping for a new career, for new challenges and successes that would ultimately lead me to a new, far more fulfilling life.

I didn't start in real estate. I grew up in rural Alabama with two parents who knew the meaning of hard work. They were both employed by the town's factories, working their fingers to the bone for little pay. They could have been negative, down on the world around them, tired and pessimistic. But instead, they willingly worked as hard as they did to give my sister and I a safe and loving home, encouraging us to surpass their lives and achievements.

"Never settle, Delarius," my parents would tell me.

That was practically our family's motto: Never Settle. My sister and I were always encouraged to get as much education as possible, to do our best and learn as many skills as we could. As a kid, I always had a vivid imagination and a mindset that I could achieve anything in life, thanks to my parents. Taking the lead in the classroom, trying new things and letting my natural curiosity lead me to discovering the narrow world around me on my own were never a problem for me.

I learned to play the piano, sang in choir and excelled in school. My parents' hard work paid off, and I attended Alabama State University, where I studied computer systems as well as business. Earning a bachelor's degree was a joy for me. I attended job fairs, networked, put myself out there in preparation for what was to come. I grew up with the dream of a world whose doors would open for me, each one its own world of possibilities and, after graduation, I was ready for those doors of corporate America to open wide.

Corporate America, unfortunately, did not feel the same way as I did. I received hundreds of rejections for job opportunities, jobs that I knew I was quite capable of performing. All of that preparation, that hard work, all of the times I did everything that experts say lead to success—none of it was working.

After several months passed, I had to come up with a Plan B. I decided to enroll in the MBA program at a local university. I

Why dream of only going half-way?

realized that I could teach piano lessons a few days a week and not interrupt my studies. I was working the plan, following the steps, putting myself out there, and this time it had to pay off. With a master's degree under my belt, the world would be my oyster. Right?

Boy, was I wrong again! By this time, I was questioning everything about myself, trying to pinpoint just where I had gone wrong. Had I missed a step? I began to think the vision I'd had for myself had led me down the wrong path. I thought people had lied to me about all the great things I could accomplish in life.

All I could do at the time was continue to teach piano lessons and fill out application after application, pounding the pavement to get interviews, to return for follow-ups—all the bullet points we're taught to achieve success. It took ten agonizing months and more rejections than I could count before I received a job offer from a large financial corporation.

Finally! At that moment I felt relief. All my hard work had paid off, and I was one step closer to what I believed was my destiny.

After a year with this company, I realized that I was still feeling unfulfilled. I was itching for a change. It hadn't been that long since I'd struggled to find work, so that memory kept me in that job where I was still drawing a paycheck. It would take several more months before I found the courage to make a change. I enrolled in

I didn't want to settle; I wanted to succeed.

real estate school with the hope of becoming a big-time agent and broker. If you're going to dream, why dream of only going half-way? Dream that you're going to reach the top!

Upon graduation, I started interviewing with real estate companies with the hope of leaving my current job, ready to embark on a new life in an industry that all signs were pointing to as booming.

Well, we all know how the housing market went bust. That happened just weeks after I got my real estate license. Several real estate companies went under as the market crashed, taking with it scores of seasoned agents and brokers.

How much more frustration could I take? My faith in myself and what I could achieve was shaken to its core.

But I realized that I had an option. I could settle, give up and let my faith in myself fall away; I could pack it in and continue to work in corporate America, unhappy and unfulfilled. Or I could take a bold step. While working at my cushy—yet unfulfilling—job, I'd managed to save a nest egg. If I couldn't be a real estate agent, maybe I could become a real estate investor on the side.

After all, there certainly was no lack of opportunity to buy homes that had been foreclosed.

I took action and purchased a property less than a mile from my parents' home. It should have been called a disaster, but I called it an opportunity. It took several weeks of constant labor, but I managed to make that property something that a family could call a home. Whoever bought that house would be able to open that front door and have the home and security they'd always envisioned.

It sold, and when I took the check from my attorney—all my profit after factoring in expenses, closing costs and such—and saw the number on that check, that level of pay was something I had never had before. In that one check was an amount greater than I'd earned working a year at my full-time job. That was the moment when my faith was completely restored. That was the moment when I knew that I *would* be successful, that I would be fortunate enough to spend my life doing something I was passionate about and that came with the bonus of making money at the same time.

Failure was not going to be an option for me. Disappointment and failure would never define me. They were simply temporary moments; they didn't determine what my whole life would be. Every time a door slammed shut in my life, it shook the foundation of my self-worth.

However, a door slammed in my face didn't mean there wasn't one that would open just down the road. It was just that *this* one wasn't opened for me. I only had to remember what my parents had taught me: Never Settle.

I was determined to have an optimistic mindset. Using the money I'd earned from that first home, I set out to purchase another property, another home that would need a total renovation, but this time I wanted to keep the property to use as a rental.

While beginning this process as a real estate investor, I was still working for the same financial corporation, but as you can probably guess, nothing about that work was truly fulfilling for me. It was time to really examine myself. What were my strengths, my skills?

I knew by then that I loved taking potential clients to see what could be their dream home, loved the whole process of buying, repairing and selling property. It left me feeling accomplished, as if I was on the road to becoming my own boss. Staying in that desk job would be settling. And that was it: I didn't want to settle; I wanted to succeed.

I knew by this time that I *could* own my life. I could do what I wanted; I didn't have to be trapped in a desk job that I didn't enjoy. I realized that the road to success isn't a straight line. There are hills and valleys, twists and turns, all manner of roadblocks that might make you want to just stop where you are and stay put. The key is to have faith that your destination is just further down that road, no matter the obstacles in your way.

Believe in that force that's pulling for you.

My faith is very important to me, something that helped me continue to get back up, to walk down the road a piece and knock on a new door. "I can do all things through Christ, who strengthens me," is my personal mantra. But this works for anyone. Call it faith, call it determination, call it Allah, or call it your own self-will, but finding that something outside of yourself will give you the strength and courage to keep pushing on day in and day out.

Your faith, your personal drive, will be put to the test regularly. You must keep focused on your dreams and goals. Don't forget your strengths. Continually remind yourself that you have a vision, you want to pursue it, and *that* is what will get you through. You have to remember who you really are, remember all you're capable of, and don't allow outside forces to influence what you know about yourself. We all have those "what if" moments, those times of self-doubt.

The key is to believe. Have faith that there is something greater, something wonderful out there. Call it whatever you like, but believe in that force that's pulling for you. Believe that success is possible. Believe that you can surpass the life you're living now.

There is more to life than the door in front of you. Keep knocking until one opens, and you'll find just how much more to the world there is when you step through it.

Delarius Madden, born and raised in Valley, Alabama now resides in Atlanta, Georgia. His MBA from Troy University helped prepare him for the wonderful business opportunity of being a successful real estate investor and entrepreneur. He recently opened his own retail store. When not engaged in public speaking or mentoring upcoming entrepreneurs in the Atlanta area, he spends his time fulfilling a life-long promise to his parents of writing his first book. Connect with Delarius at www.delarius.com.

DIANE F. SMITH

LIVE OUTSIDE THE BOX

How many "never buts" have you heard this month? This year? In your lifetime? "Never buts" are usually some version of this: "You'll never be anything but a… fill in the blank." Usually a statement like that is preceded or followed by, "Why bother?" Why bother trying, or dreaming, or setting a goal? Why bother working hard, or investing in yourself (or others)? Why bother improving yourself, educating yourself? Why bother growing? After all, you'll never be anything but…

Sometimes the "why bother" is implied. Other times, we only hear "why bother," and the "never but" is implied. And sometimes we only hear derisive laughter or see a roll of the eyes, even an angry glare. It's there, the limiting statement that can infiltrate your brain and cause you to put your dreams away and stop trying. It's easy to let other people's negative beliefs *about* you, and low expectations *for* you, become reality. It's easy because usually these statements come from people we love and value. "Never buts" can take on a life of their own, but they always lie.

I was the product of a "shotgun marriage" that ended in divorce, followed by years of fighting about custody, child support and visitation, almost always initiated by my grandmothers. One weekend, I went to court-ordered visitation with my father, who was living with his mother at the time. His mother always asked me to do chores around her house, and I did them. She never thanked me, or showed me any affection. As a result, I was not close to her.

I was outside playing baseball when my grandmother called me in and asked me to mop the kitchen floor.

I said, "I don't mop the kitchen floor at home where I live and I'm not going to mop yours."

With that, my grandmother kicked me hard in the butt and said, "You'll never be anything in life but a cleaning woman."

Sobbing, I gathered my things to leave. Concerned that I would report to my mother, my father and grandmother tried to convince me to stay, but I left her house and ran. I was in shock, so hurt that she would physically abuse me. My eyes were so flooded with tears I could barely find my way home.

When I arrived at home and told my mother what had happened, the drama began.

Livid, my mother said, "You did the right thing coming home. I'm so sorry that happened to you."

Within three weeks we were back in family court again. The judge, whose daughter was a close friend of mine, asked to speak to me privately in his chambers. As he had been the judge on all court matters related to my family, I had been in that room many times.

**"You'll never be anything in life
but a cleaning woman."**

He asked me to tell him in my own words what happened, and when I did he asked, "How do you think you should have been treated?"

I could tell that he empathized with my deep sense of confusion and feelings of rejection, and I could see that he understood I felt beaten down and unloved.

In a small voice I said, "Judge, she kicked me, as if I were some sort of animal, or someone other than me, her grandchild. I never want to go back there again."

My grandmother's statement: "You'll never be anything in life but a cleaning woman" still echoed through my mind as the judge explained that he would limit the visitation further, so I didn't have to go as frequently or stay as long. I felt helpless.

Then he said, "I'm sorry you have to go through this, Diane. I hope you grow up to be a nice young lady."

That event shaped my life. In the months that followed, I thought too often about the physical and emotional abuse I received from my father's mother. Many nights I couldn't sleep; the other nights I had nightmares that I grew up to be a cleaning woman. Sometimes I would wake up crying and my mother would soothe me, holding me in her arms. Over and over again, she told me, "You will grow up to be a successful person."

I was on a mission to be a success in my work life.

One day, after months of affirmations and reassurances from my mother, it finally dawned on me: *I am not going to be anyone's cleaning woman. Whatever I do in life, I will be successful.*

From that moment forward I made the decision that I would not let my grandmother—or anyone—tell me what I was going to be. I knew I would amount to something, that no matter what I chose to do in life, I would do well. I was on a mission to be a success in my work life, and I would have nothing less.

As a child, I had a close relationship with my grandfather, my mother's father. In fact, I called him "Daddy." He took me to baseball games, to the circus, to wrestling matches. He taught me how to hit and field a baseball and bought me my first baseball mitt. I loved him so much.

One day, when I was about twelve years old, he sat me down for a talk.

"I'm not well," he said. "I'm going to die soon."

I didn't believe him, and told him so—he seemed to be in perfectly good health.

He just looked at me and said, "Promise me you will go to college, and become the first person in our family to earn a college degree."

"I promise," I replied.

After that conversation, I felt strange. *Why did Daddy have that talk with me?* When he tried to bring it up again, I said, "Daddy, don't talk to me about dying. You're going to live forever. You'll live to see me graduate from college."

He died six weeks later from a sudden massive stroke. I was crushed. Daddy was my everything. I couldn't eat, or sleep, and for days I spent all hours crying uncontrollably.

Somehow, Daddy knew his time was short, and his last wish was that I graduate from college. After that, I was certain my path to success required that I graduate from college. Daddy had given

"Promise me you will go to college."

me the map I needed to begin my walk on the path to success. I was single-minded. I studied hard and stayed focused. I never had to say "no" to drugs, or other trouble, because it never crossed my mind. The only thing on my mind was getting good grades so I could make good on my promise to Daddy.

When I was accepted to college, my mother worked hard to help pay my tuition. The "never buts" started again, family members and friends telling her, "Why are you paying for college? Diane's going to meet a man there, and she's never going to be anything but a housewife. You're just wasting your money."

There it was—"why bother" and "never but."

Now, there's nothing wrong with being a housewife, or a cleaning woman, for that matter. The naysayers may even have meant well. But for me, it felt as though they were trying to define my life, and that just wasn't going to happen. My mother, who had been my greatest inspiration and support—drilling me with quizzes, helping me research potential careers, keeping me on the straight-and-narrow—she believed in me. She wouldn't listen to the "never buts," and neither would I. Even my high school guidance counselor gave me a "never but"—"You'll never reach any career higher than a teacher," she'd said one day. Again, she may have meant well, but she could not define me.

To ease my mother's financial burden, I finished college in three years. When I decided a few years later to get my master's degree within one year, my department head said, "You can't get a master's degree in one year."

I smiled at him and said: "Watch me."

At the time I was completing my master's, my mother was dying of cancer. Despite working full-time and taking care of my toddler son, I was motivated to finish in one year so she could see me walk across the stage and graduate with honors—and I did. My mother was in a wheelchair at the time, weakened by her illness. When I

I had lived up to the promise.

walked across the stage she stood up from her chair and clapped and jumped up and down as best she could. She was beyond happy. I had fulfilled the hopes and aspirations she and Daddy had for me. I had done the unthinkable, what people told me I could not do.

Standing on that stage, looking at my mother's beaming face, I was ecstatic. I had defied everyone in my life who had told me I couldn't do something—all the people who came at me with "never buts" and "why bothers." And I had lived up to the promise my mother and grandfather had for me. I lived and thrived outside the box others tried to put me in. There was no stopping me now.

I continued to be a trailblazer—the first person in my family to own a home, to invest in properties, to build a successful stock portfolio, to take on key management positions, and on and on. Along the way I had failures and disappointments, but I never let them deter me from my goals.

I used to look at failures negatively, but I have come to understand that failure is an experience you are supposed to learn from in order to move on, to grow and to become the person you intend to be. There are no failures; there are only experiences, a response from the universe to remind you that you have something to learn or realize *before* you can move forward.

When you fail, it's easy to believe the "never buts" you were once told. In the aftermath, failure may appear to be proof that the naysayers were right, which can lead you down a path that ends in giving up. Simply by reframing your definition of failure, understanding that it is a learning experience, not an ending or a judgment, you will be able to continue to ignore the "never buts" and stay the course to prosperity.

Find the lesson in failure, first by recognizing that *is* a learning experience. Then, acknowledge that it was supposed to happen, because all experiences come from the universe. Once you do this, the lesson will become obvious. Perhaps you have been making bad decisions that are not helpful. Maybe it's time to reevaluate your priorities. Whatever the reason, it's important to remain objective, rather than emotional. Only then can you benefit from the experience and move forward with success. It's not important where you start; it's important where you finish.

Don't let people define you; you define who and what you are. Live outside the box others expect you to live in. And, in the pursuit of goals, never tell yourself no, or listen to the "never buts." Living life like this allows the universe to align with your purpose and move you forward on the path to success.

You are who you are, not who others say you are. Never forget.

Diane F. Smith is a professional manager, entrepreneur, business consultant, public speaker and author. Diane was born, raised and educated in Ohio and received an MA Degree in urban planning. As a professional manager, she managed field activity for over twelve hundred personnel in one hundred twenty-five offices for a large Federal agency. With her personal staff, she had a proven record of accepting problem employees and turning them into productive staff by giving them opportunities to start over and treating them with respect. Her organization was known as the "go to" office for new organizational ideas and "out of the box" management tools.

Diane travelled extensively to assess field performance and to deliver speeches, for which she received numerous awards in recognition of her exemplary performance. Concomitantly, she owned and operated three antique stores—one in Maryland, one in Virginia and one in Washington, D.C.

After she left the Federal agency, her business consultancy was born when several entrepreneurs asked Diane for assistance in setting up their businesses. She guides clients in areas of business organization, marketing, product development and strategic planning. She is currently writing a book about her triumphant journey facing a major life challenge. Connect with Diane at www.DianeFSmith.com.

RICHARD BROWN, PHD

MAXIMIZE YOUR CHANCE FOR GREATNESS

One Christmas, early in my career as a healthcare administrator, I took a seasonal job at Toys "R" Us. I was between jobs, having left my last position as Chief Operating Officer (COO) at an ambulatory healthcare facility in Kansas City due to a disagreement with my Chief Executive Officer (CEO) about management philosophy. Being a healthcare administrator, is similar to being a professional football coach. If you are let go as the head coach in one town, you have to find employment in another town; you just don't go to a different healthcare facility in the same town.

Because six months is about the time it takes to find a new job in the healthcare administration field, and because I needed a job to support my wife and two children, I applied for the job at Toys "R" Us. On my application, I did not indicate my three academic degrees: a bachelor's degree, a master's degree and a PhD. I was afraid of the look I would surely get from the hiring manager if he knew about my academic and career history and I did not want to be told I was overqualified.

As I unloaded box cars on the night shift for minimum wage, I thought I had lived up to the prediction of my high school guidance counselor. I could still hear her voice tell me, "Your grades are so bad you should seek a career working with your hands."

At the time, I viewed high school as a place to have fun. I wasn't thinking about my future. The thought of a future limited to manual labor jobs caused me to say, "Wait a minute. I'm smarter than that. I just haven't been applying myself. I can do better."

The guidance counselor's prediction was the wake-up call I needed to start taking school seriously and apply myself. I went on to get excellent grades and go to college and, at age twenty-nine, had an experience that determined my destiny. While completing

I could not let this experience define me.

my residency at a hospital in Atlanta, I had the opportunity to witness an open heart surgery. For six hours I watched intently from the observation room. I was extremely impressed with the science of the surgery, the skill, the precision and the patience of the personnel—and the miracle of the process.

I decided from that day forward I would become as knowledgeable and skilled at managing healthcare services as the physicians, nurses and technicians who performed open heart surgery. I felt it was my duty, out of respect for the serious life-and-death work that healthcare providers do every day to save lives and prevent illness, to study hard and become the best healthcare administrator possible.

And yet there I was, years later, seeming to live up to the limited expectations of my high school guidance counselor as I hauled boxes of toys all night long. But I knew I could not let this experience define me. Anyone who looked at me stacking inventory at three a.m. might assume my options were limited, but there was no shame in my job at Toys "R" Us, and it was not a position in which I would be forced to remain. It was a moment, a temporary setback. I would prevail and make good on my commitment to healthcare.

I did find a new job in my field four months later and, in my thirty five-year career as a healthcare administrator, I know I fulfilled the promise I made to myself in high school and the commitment I made when I witnessed the miracle of open heart surgery.

A second turning point in my quest to become the CEO of a healthcare organization was when I became the Chief of the Bureau of Special Healthcare Needs with in the Missouri State Health Department. There, I managed ten offices located throughout the state that provided health services for children born with disabilities. The Bureau consisted of two hundred employees and had a budget of fourteen million dollars. It was there that I gained confidence and realized the knowledge, experience and continuing education in the field of healthcare administration had paid off.

Out of the culmination of my career experiences, several concepts for success in the healthcare business, have emerged. I wish to share one such concept. I integrated it into the thinking

**We must strive for perfection
at every juncture.**

of employees and permeated it throughout every facility that we occupied while at the Charles Drew Healthcare Center (CDHC), a federally qualified health center (FQHC).

A plaque on the wall has a slogan made up of three phrases. These phrases identify the objective of all of the employees that work for the CDHC. This objective can be recited by every employee who has worked in the organization for more than thirty days.

It represents the thinking to which I attribute the success that we had in the healthcare business during the twelve years of my watch as CEO.

The objective of all of the employees was the same, whether they cut the grass and emptied the trash, or served as appointment schedulers or medical and dental assistants, or patient advocates, or lab technicians, or behavioral health specialists, or language interpreters, or as nurse practitioners, or dentists, or physicians. I call this objective the Three Ms, which are the first words of each phrase, maximize, maximize, minimize:

Maximizing patient encounters has to do with encouraging families from the community to come to the office to see a physician, dentist, midlevel or behavioral health practitioner. At each office visit, we can educate them about living healthy, risk-free lives. We can teach them about their chronic disease, be it diabetes, high blood pressure or heart disease or about their pregnancy or depression. We can encourage them to develop self-management goals to help prevent or control their chronic diseases.

Maximizing patient satisfaction has to do with ensuring that each patient has a pleasant social experience. Patients may not be able to recognize that they have received healthcare that is of high quality, but they can see and feel how well they were embraced by staff. So, we want each patient to leave the health center with a smile and with hope that life will get better. Additionally, happy patients will return for follow up visits, which improves their health status and improves our financial bottom line.

Minimizing errors and inefficiencies has to do with making sure that we try all that is within our power to eliminate mistakes. To be perfect is nearly impossible, but in the healthcare services business, the public expects and deserves nothing less. It is a life or death matter. Mistakes must be kept to a minimum. We had more than thirty-three thousand visits in 2013. Because the system of providing healthcare services is so complicated and has so many moving parts, we must strive for perfection at every juncture. I am proud that we were cited by consultants for Health Resources Services Administration as having one of the best quality improvement systems among the hundreds of health centers visited throughout the country.

The concept of the Three Ms, while developed out of my healthcare management experience, is transferable to any business to increase the likelihood of success. Individually, these words are simple and uncomplicated. But used collectively as a way to think about how to succeed, they become very powerful and can accelerate the speed at which you can accomplish your personal or business objectives.

Your goal or mission may be to achieve a social, personal, business, management or entrepreneurial objective. It matters not whether you are selling services or producing a particular product, the concept will apply. To be successful, you must participate in daily activity that maximizes the thing that you want to accomplish. You must maximize sales, clients, partners or distribution of products. When maximizing your goal, you must think not only locally, about your city and state, and nationally, but worldwide. Never has it been so easy to obtain maximum exposure to large numbers of people than in the current Internet and social media era. Two-thirds of the people on this planet are connected via social media and cell phones. Somebody on earth will purchase what ever it is that you have to sell.

Maximize, maximize, minimize.

Maximizing and exercising excellent customer service is undisputed as a key element to the success of most ventures. Customer satisfaction is an increasing determinant of market advantage. Customers, clients, or partners must be kept happy, satisfied, impressed, or they will seek satisfaction elsewhere. Customers who have a pleasant, enjoyable experience keep returning for more. When they do, your business grows and thrives and your dreams can be realized.

Minimizing errors and inefficiencies is another undisputable element of success. Be it personal, socially, or in business, no one tolerates mistakes very well. In the healthcare business, mistakes can cause injuries and death. In business, mistakes can cost money. In life, they can cost love, relationships and family.

Examples of mistakes that took place include the Malaysian flight 370 that disappeared over the Indian Ocean and the ferryboat that capsized in South Korea, as well as the massive automobile recall by General Motors due to defective ignition switches. Such errors and inefficiencies hurt the businesses financially and clearly cost the lives of many people.

Maximizing your product, services or dreams; maximizing customer service; and minimizing errors and inefficiencies is the best daily formula for success in realizing the attainment of your dreams. You may find yourself in a temporary situation as I did the Christmas season I worked for Toys "R" Us, wondering if the naysayers of your past were right and concerned that you had failed, or failed one too many times. However, if you remain diligent and consistent in your approach toward your dreams— toward greatness—you maximize your chances for success and claim the destiny you so rightfully deserve.

Richard L. Brown, Ph.D., FACHE, is CEO of Lee Brown and Associates, his health services management consulting company. Under Brown's leadership, healthcare organizations have experienced tremendous growth and change in medical, dental and behavioral health services. A fitness center was developed at CDHC in 2010 to provide a place for employees, patients and the community to participate in exercise activity. He often uses humor to motivate and inspire audiences to maximize their chances for greatness.

Dr. Brown's career spans over thirty-five years of administrative experience in a variety of health services organizations, both private and non-profit, that served vulnerable populations. He has served in the management and leadership positions of assistant administrator/ COO of an acute care hospital; administrator of a rural ambulatory healthcare center, an FQHC; administrator of a home health agency; COO of an urban ambulatory healthcare facility, an FQHC, that operated a health maintenance organization, as well as bureau chief of a state health department.

Dr. Brown is skilled at interacting effectively with a wide variety of stakeholders, including advocacy organizations, state and local government and philanthropic organizations as well as healthcare providers. He is strong in managing program budgets; ensuring financial accountability, quality improvement and staff and physician satisfaction, as well as maintaining operational and performance standards. Dr. Brown is a seasonal administrator with proven leadership, organizational and interpersonal skills.

Nationally he has served as the founder and president of two local chapters of the National Association of Health Services Executives (NAHSE). He also served on the NAHSE Board of Directors from 1987-2001 and has participated as an active member of NAHSE for the past thirty-five years. In October 2006, Dr. Brown was the recipient of the Senior Health Services Executive of the Year Award.

Additionally, Dr. Brown has served ten years as assistant or adjunct professor at three universities. He served on the national boards of the Institute for Diversity in Health Management. He is a Fellow of the American College of Healthcare Executives. He has published a book chapter on long-term care and articles on health services administration. He has a bachelor's degree in sociology from Missouri University-St. Louis, a master's degree in health services administration from St. Louis University, and a doctorate in adult and continuing education from Florida State University. Connect with Dr. Brown at www.LeeBrownAndAssociates.com.

JESSICA ROBINSON

CONSCIOUS COURAGE

A few years ago, while trekking in Nepal, I became very ill after my first meal and couldn't keep anything down. It was forty-eight hours of feeling horrible. Scared, not sure if this sickness would end, and exhausted, my body spent from repeated vomiting, I finally slept. It was then that I had a dream I will never forget.

My grandmother, my mother's mom, had passed nearly six years earlier. I found myself at a gathering in her sixty-year-old house. The wood floors were inexplicably covered by white carpeting. We were getting ready for a big party, though it was still early; only a handful of people had arrived.

While we talked quietly amongst ourselves, my grandmother came up the stairs. She looked beautiful! Her gray-white hair was short, and she was wearing a fitted purple dress with a short train. It looked as though she was floating, and it seemed she looked at me as if I was the only person in the room.

As she approached me, it was as if the room parted for her. She looked directly at me, glowing, smiling her all-knowing Mona Lisa smile.

I hugged her and said, "You look amazing!"

She paused, looked deeply into my eyes and said softly, "You can come with me now, or you can stay."

Intuitively, I knew the correct answer. I looked back at her and said, "I will stay."

Her face calm and pleasant, she replied, "You have much more work left to do."

Shortly after that, I woke up in our wooden cabin. My boyfriend's twin bed opposite mine was empty since he had already left for breakfast. I was dehydrated and exhausted, so I just lay there, thinking about what my dream could mean. *I have more work to do. What work am I meant to do?*

Then suddenly, I knew.

Seven years before the dream I had about my grandma, I was starting my second year in graduate school. I was at the student health center for my yearly checkup, anxiously waiting for the nurse to return. I could hear the distant voices of people sitting next door and out in the waiting room. My heart beat a little faster. I wondered, *Why did she insist on a urine sample?* I checked my phone, but there was still no call from my boyfriend.

I failed as mother; I failed as a daughter.

The nurse finally walked in and closed the door. I sat up straight, ready to leave so I could finish some work before class.

She said, "You're pregnant," in a scolding tone.

Both what she said and the way she said it caught me off guard. She continued speaking, but I couldn't make out what she was saying. I was sitting in an office, looking at the paper-littered desk, the bookcase full of medical references and then the white wall. It's always a white wall. I could hardly breathe.

"This can't be happening," I said to myself. "This is not real." As she continued to talk, I felt a lump in my throat, uneasiness in my chest and tears in my eyes. She stopped talking. Silence filled the room, and all I could see was the look on her disapproving face. Not knowing what she said, but not wanting to give her the satisfaction of seeing me cry, I got up to leave.

I walked out the main entrance, and the sun blinded me, while the breeze cooled the tears on my cheek. Naturally a private person, I could not hide my vulnerability in that moment. Crying, I dialed my boyfriend's number and sneaked into the alley behind the health center. "I am pregnant," I told him.

It was my biggest fear, and my self-fulfilling prophecy was coming to life. The nurse knew that nearly six weeks earlier I had been pregnant with a different fetus and that this was my third

No matter one's situation, there is a way through.

pregnancy in nineteen months. I could not imagine this. I could not have predicted that this would be my life. I was scared to have a baby and for my child's future. There was terrorizing confusion, a raping of my spirit and an unending desire for what I wanted, and didn't want, with my partner—and, of course, the shame I felt at being with child out of wedlock, with no money and no health insurance. Loved ones calling me a "loser with no common sense" made me wonder if they were right. Would a woman with common sense be in this situation? I couldn't answer that question and, subsequently, I couldn't summon the strength to fight for my child.

I failed as mother; I failed as a daughter. I believed I was worth nothing. I was completely broken. I truly thought that when I walked down the street, even the plants wept as I passed. How could I have been so unhealthy? I had made the same mistakes over and over. How could I have traveled the world, yet be so lost on every step of that journey and not know it? Where was my self-respect, and when did I lose it?

I could not tell anyone except two cousins who supported me through the process. I was thankful for their love and generosity and for creating a judgment-free environment. They both listened.

One told me at dinner one night, "It wasn't what happened that actually mattered, but how I responded to this going forward."

I had learned: No matter one's situation, there is a way through. Something greater was waiting for me.

As is true for many young girls, it took me a while to find my way in the world and build confidence. I was unsure of myself and had trouble finding my voice in high school and through college, mostly spurred by my acute need for perfection and having the "disease to please." As many people do, I had trouble accepting myself, because I was still trying to figure out who I was versus what I thought others wanted me to be.

Failure is a natural part of the ebb and flow of life, as is success. We, as spiritual beings, have to learn to adapt to that fact and start to trust in our own intuitions. Not being attached to an outcome can be as important as what we learn on the journey and what we can offer others in return.

**Every being should have a true
sense of personal freedom.**

Over the years, I have spent more and more time on the topics of failure and building personal security and confidence, not only because I have failed many times myself personally and professionally, but also because I have been fascinated by the resiliency of the human spirit and believe the answer we are looking for is within ourselves.

I have spent time studying philosophy and spiritualty and the lives of incredibly successful men and women who have publicly failed and yet have gone on to have their most brilliant successes. Reading about people like Walt Disney, Henry Ford and Albert Einstein, who by all accounts should not have succeeded, gave me hope.

Ford had a third grade education, went bankrupt and didn't know when America won its independence or the names any of our founding fathers. Disney was fired from his first job for not being creative enough and went bankrupt before finally achieving success.

Winston Churchill, though he won the Nobel Prize for literature, was not well regarded politically and lost every election until he became Prime Minister of England during World War II. Abraham Lincoln suffered from depression and lost six congressional and senatorial races until his presidential election.

Even Oprah Winfrey was once fired and told she was "unfit for TV." I studied more women who openly discussed challenges similar to those I faced: Billie Jean King, Alice Walker, Sherri Sheppard, Rebecca Walker, Chris Evert, Ava Gardner, Gloria Steinem and Whoopi Goldberg to name a few. I truly respect their talents, including those of Maya Angelou, who was a prostitute and a madam. Her story shows that the choices one makes in the past need not stop you from living a future that includes your true mission of giving your gifts to the world.

The ultimate lesson was for me to learn to have conscious courage and first simply see the truth and take responsibility and acknowledge that a different choice could have been made. However, in other situations, it's possible another choice could not have been made. In those cases, it's important to forgive yourself and move forward, instead of holding on to secrets that will slowly weaken your health or assassinate you. That also included honoring the pain felt by others like my family, my boyfriend and others.

The path of forgiveness is one of trust. The most common betrayal we all experience is the one against ourselves. Courage is the antidote we need to fight through to joy and love. We have to be the revolutionaries, what I call "Ferocious Beings of Courage," of our own lives. We have to revolt against who we were and then we have to reestablish a relationship of trust so that there is no choice but for transformation to occur.

As part of the healing process, I had a strong sense of service. Volunteering was a medicine of its own and helped me heal my broken spirit. Not only do we learn through service how we can contribute our best selves to the world, but we remember that we have value only we can give. I needed to make the most of the life I had left and make a difference in the world. I started to volunteer at an after-school activities center for students who were impacted by HIV/AIDS—either they had the virus, or someone in their family did. At the most painful time in my life, that opened my eyes to a new type of suffering. Through service, I learned every human being, including me, has the power to redeem their lives.

It wasn't until seven years later, after feeling immense love and gratitude with my children through various meditations, that I was able to truly forgive myself and love who I am now and know my children are with me every part of every day. When I simply changed my perspective from that of a human being to that of a conscious spiritual being, I had the deep understanding that my children had forgiven me the moment it happened. The ultimate learning for me was to create a sense of personal security only I could provide and to remember my undeniable strength as a *wild ferocious being of courage.*

Discovering the best version of myself helped me reveal my true strengths, which gave me the confidence to lead with courage. Accepting that I'm not "perfect" has allowed my spirit to blossom, to accept all that I have to offer, flaws and all, as a diverse complex female, results-driven humanist and inspiring, yet unique, leader. Leading with courage and confidence, I founded Conscious Courage Living and PurePoint International, two ideas that changed the way I contribute to the world.

Every being should have a true sense of personal freedom; *every* soul is important. You have total power and you are as important as any other person. You can benefit from life experiences by not defining yourself by your limitations. Reorient yourself to a new perspective on your past, and never let anyone beat you down until you cannot make your own decisions about you and your life—not even *you*. When in pain don't wait for a miracle, be a miracle!

Conscious courage is a focus on being deliberate while taking steps to do what you know you have been called to do. As Nelson Mandela stated, it's not about overcoming fear. It's feeling the fear and doing it anyway. It's living your life in the most authentic way possible and moving forward, making decisions with your heart and mind aligned. It's about surrender to your purpose, though not knowing what the future holds or being able to make sense of it. It's having a faith and an understanding that surrendering to courage will lead to authenticity and to living the life only you were meant to live.

As I lay in that twin bed in Nepal, waking up from the dream about my grandmother, I didn't know immediately, but over time, I knew my contribution would intersect with my work experience

It's feeling the fear and doing it anyway.

in safety and security, with my personal experience learning to respect my body, with my passion for women's and girls' issues and with my spiritual mission of raising levels of consciousness and areas of the human spirit. That mission evolved to focus specifically on creating a safer, more secure global environment for women to raise their children, provide for their families, receive an education and live their lives as they choose, without fear or intimidation. This means increasing women's own sense of personal security and protecting their bodies.

Similarly to Maslow's hierarchy of needs, a sense of being personally secure is the most important thing for human beings, especially women. The role women play in creating a more peaceful world by elevating human consciousness is a direct result of increasing safety and security that allows each individual to speak their truth without fear of consequences. Personal security is one of the most important things in a relationship, because it's about being accepted for who you are.

As scary as it is to tell this story, I couldn't waste time caring about what people think. *There is too much work to be done!* I heard David Wheeler, parent of one of the children killed at the Sandy Hook school shooting, say, "It doesn't matter what you expect from life; what matters is what life expects from you. And what you have to do is find yourself out of the dark." I am not my past, and I have an unwritten future that only I can design through my vision. I needed this experience to become the person I am today and to appreciate and accept the lessons of love and honor.

I believe, for each of us, our soul has a plan and a specific lesson our spirit needs to learn in this human life to grow and evolve. Our ability to transcend from where we were to where we are going is a reflection of this process. True self-love only comes from within, and we have to start where we are with courage: courage to look at the things we despise about ourselves, with the hope that we have the strength to change it. My goal is now to continue with this human experience and allow my spirit to live its mission and give myself humbly and compassionately to each person I meet.

What's most important is not my story of what occurred, but how I was able to come back from that and be the person I am today: confident, full of self-love and love for others, full of gratitude and compassion, successful in my career and life, global influencer, business leader, nonprofit leader, empowerer and social entrepreneur. The healing process was nearly eight years of challenging me to face the truth about who I was and who I wanted to be, finding refuge in faith and eventually learning how to love myself. Having new values and a sense of mission from eight years of hard work has gotten me to where I am today.

And yes, to quote my grandmother, "I have much more work to do."

Jessica Robinson is a "Conscious Courage Activist," working internationally at the intersection of tech entrepreneurship, strategic partnerships and safety and security. Through Conscious Courage Living, Jessica provides life purpose and career coaching designed to help individuals find the courage to create peace within themselves, thereby creating a movement of "Ferocious Beings of Courage" around the world. As the founder of PurePoint International, a New York-based company dedicated to increasing personal security among all individuals, particularly women, globally, Jessica consults on safety and security matters and is developing technology solutions for personal security concerns. Before founding PurePoint International, Jessica spent eight years in assets protection in corporate America, concentrating on security, internal and external theft investigations and emergency response, and in her last position leading and supporting a six-hundred-million-dollar business. She also collaborated in implementing an enterprise-wide strategy based on public/private partnerships and established community initiatives with local, state and federal public safety partners.

Jessica currently serves on the board of World Pulse, an international nonprofit that lifts and unites women's voices to accelerate their impact on the world, is a Director of Strategic Partnerships with the Emerging Global Leadership Circle with Impact Leadership 21 and serves on the United Nations Women Committee for Public/Private Partnerships. Jessica received a BS in law enforcement and justice administration with honors from Western Illinois University. She received her master's degree in public and international affairs, with a focus on security and intelligence studies from the University of Pittsburgh and earned an East Asian studies certificate. In 2011, Jessica completed a certificate in business excellence from Columbia Business School Executive Education and the Institute for Personal Leadership. Jessica became a Fellow with the Women's Leadership Institute at the Impact Center in Washington, D.C. in 2011, and a Fellow with Impact Leadership 21 in 2014. Connect with Jessica at www.The-PurePoint.com and www. ConsciousCourageLiving.com.

NYA REYNOLDS

SCREAMING ON MUTE

There are many ways to lose your voice. We let stress and sadness get in our way and dampen our spirits. We don't have to do that—we can find the love within ourselves and find our voices again.

It was a sunny Tuesday morning as I drove my father's purple 96 Honda Accord, listening to the Tom Joyner radio show. I passed by the Hampton Coliseum, admiring its beautiful architecture, and started my journey down 64 West. I began thinking about the past weekend, the Fourth of July. My boyfriend had not been faithful and I knew it. Yet I allowed him to spend the night with me and agreed to drive him to work the next morning. "What was I thinking?" I asked myself over and over. I thought I was happy and having fun. But when he wasn't with me to watch fireworks, I felt awful.

I passed a rest stop, which let me know I was half-way home. Then I heard a loud *bump*. The steering wheel jerked out of my control, and the car spun around. I screamed as the car slid down off the highway and hit a tree before caroming off and resting on another, just above a deep pond.

The right side of my head hit the passenger window, knocking me unconscious, and my right hip shifted. My left leg was bleeding. My brain was swelling with blood, and I was flown in a helicopter to Richmond's Medical College of Virginia. Twice I pulled out my breathing tube, and once more when I was in the ICU, until finally they let me do without it. I woke up screaming, "I'm late for work." My mother was next to me, telling me I couldn't go anywhere.

I was in the hospital. I was moved to a regular room, with a roommate who had a shaved head. Instantly I was afraid they'd have to shave my hair—luckily they just cut along the parts of my microbraids during the emergency surgery to relieve the swelling in my brain.

A week later I was out of the hospital. Recovery started slowly, with limping, headaches, slurring and memory loss. I didn't realize how badly I'd been hurt.

My mom recently returned home after being institutionalized due to self-medicating her bipolar disorder. She struggled with the

The steering wheel jerked out of my control.

pain her choices caused. She couldn't understand why I wanted to be with a man who cheated on me. He was a sailor with three children from a previous relationship. My mother could not stand the sight of him and envisioned much more for me. Yet I loved him and I enjoyed his company. He would brighten my day when came to visit on the weekends.

Two weeks after my release I started getting sore throats, so inflamed that I could barely breathe. I stayed the course, though—I took lozenges and gargled salt water and vinegar. Nothing helped, and it became harder to take a breath. One night I really couldn't, so my boyfriend drove me to the hospital, and I was admitted immediately. The doctors gave me something to help me get my breath, and left me alone—their mistake.

Refusing to use the bedpan. I went to the bathroom and, before I could get back to bed, almost passed out from having no breath; my head was swimming and my vision was blacking. And I hallucinated—I saw a great stone wall with moving pictures of a smiling hula girl.

I stumbled and I said to my boyfriend, "I'm tripping."

Soon enough the doctors came and gave me something to sleep. But the next morning, I found out the truth about my sore throat—I had scar tissue so severe that oxygen was too heavy to breathe. It was like having a coffee stirrer for a throat, instead of a quarter-sized windpipe. I needed a tracheotomy to live.

I called all my friends and family, but only a few showed up. I was scared and felt alone—my boyfriend had left; my mother was the only one there in the end. So I was bitter and rude and took it out on everything. I wanted their love and they weren't giving it.

After surgery, I woke with my hands tied again and my voice gone. I had a tube in my throat, and my mother had disappeared, forcing my father to come get me. I heard the nurses whispering about it, and I was embarrassed and felt lonely and unloved. Everyone knew something wasn't right. But my dad came, and my mother wasn't with him. So they just showed him how to care for my tracheotomy tube while I wrote notes to my dad about how my mother probably went to drugs because she couldn't deal with seeing me like this. My dad wouldn't let me blame myself, though.

She came home that night, apologetic, yet depressed, which increased her ongoing pain. She refused to take the medication prescribed for her bipolar disorder and returned to self-medication. This pattern only continued; she'd come home in drug-fueled rages that hung over our house like lightning. It was always there, just waiting for us.

But nothing stayed certain with me. My health only declined. My drainage was tinged with blood, and soon it was discovered that there was more scar tissue below the tracheotomy tube. My doctors wanted to send me to Boston and agreed to fly me up, since the long drive was dangerous. And I would be making it alone— I'd broken up with my boyfriend, and my mother was seldom to be found.

The night before I went to Boston I was lonely and scared. I reflected on how I got to that place, with no one with me. My friends were gone; my family was too busy for me. My mother wasn't there when I needed her; my father wanted to be but couldn't. I was alone. I had no one there to love me.

I couldn't even scream. I tried; oh, I tried. I screamed to God, silent, "I want to live! I want to live!" No one could hear me. But prayers don't need a voice to be heard, and so I prayed and I reflected and the next day I woke to the sun shining down on my smile.

My entire flight, I listened to one song: "Through With Love" by Destiny's Child. I decided I was through with my cheating boyfriend's love and the pain of my mothers's antics. I was through trying to find love outside of myself—I would find it within. I would find it in my love for my father, who could not go into the operating room with me even though he wanted to. I would find it in God, who protected me, held me close like a child to a mother's bosom.

I wanted my mother's touch, a stroke of the hair, but she wasn't there. I couldn't find comfort outside of myself, so I could only look inside.

When I arrived in Boston, I was taken to the hospital. And the doctors there were amazed with my smile. "You're still smiling with all you've been through?" they asked.

**Too often we look outside
of ourselves for love.**

I nodded yes with bright eyes, because smiling made me feel better and my spirit shine. Although my body was ailing, my broken spirit was slowly being mended from the inside out.

That's where love really is—within you. And the first step to healing is to evaluate and acknowledge the source of that love. Be brutally honest with yourself. Ask yourself, *why was I created?* What makes you, a being of flesh and meat and bone, move? What is that spirit; what makes it happiest? It may be nature, or dancing, or reading or video games. What makes you happiest inside yourself? Let yourself be simple—for example, I love the smell of crayons and I make myself happy by coloring. What makes you happy?

Too often we look outside of ourselves for love. We look to our children or our husbands. We look to our work or to fans. But when you don't start within, you don't know what you're worthy of. Are you willing to work and sacrifice for that self-love? Can you say no to distraction and focus on action?

I did. I ended up with an electrical voice box that made me sound like a robot. I remember my cousin joking, "You can't violate the machine, cussing and such." I did anyway, of course. And I

I kept myself safe and put myself first.

continued my treatment and had major reconstructive surgery. I remember I had to get my license renewed for my twenty-fifth birthday and I had to get my picture taken with surgical tape still on my throat. I didn't care—I smiled anyway.

A team of students had to do a SWOT analysis on a company, and each person had to orally present their part. My professor expected me to do my part. So I stood in front of the class, nervously looking at my peers. My stomach was in knots; with a big smile, I let my eyes sparkle. With the assistance of the electro-larynx I spoke as clearly as I could. We received an A.

One year and six months later, I whispered without the voice box to help me. My doctor told me to practice. And I practiced and practiced. "Thank you Lord," I said, over and over, until a choppy, raspy voice could say those words.

But I went further than just getting my voice back for school. I said *no* to the pool of things that wanted to keep me from committing. When I started graduate school I was determined to continue no matter what. I pushed through and kept going. I even took my computer with me on some of my many trips to Boston, doing my homework and even submitting my work to my professors long-distance. They worked with me and let me work online as I completed the tail end of my MBA.

I kept myself safe and put myself first. I stayed with the goals and dreams I wanted to achieve and I achieved them. My mother cleaned up her act, dealt with her pain and went back to school. She got her MBA, and we mended our relationship. She was right about the boyfriend. I made sacrifices—staying up to study, eating healthy, exercising, maintaining my sanity. I visualized my success and graduated to a corporate internship program. My entire internship team was like family and joined me in graduation. We left no man behind, and we exemplified the knowledge we'd been taught and put it into the world as professionals, achieving what few people achieve. And I attained and maintained a professional career with the government.

I felt the love inside then, because without God being there, without the sacrifices, I wouldn't have made it. I had to look deep within and *know*—I can and I will. And I did.

Nya Reynolds is a double graduate from Saint Leo University with a BA and MBA in business management, specializing in training. She is building a business that assists clients in evaluating and discovering their confidence. She also advocates for people with disabilities, specifically onset disabilities caused by trauma and disease. Connect with Nya at www.FBGEnterprize.com.

DAPHNE CLARKE-HUDSON, PHD

YOUR SONG WILL GUIDE YOU THROUGH

Many female prisoners have gathered to hear me speak at the women's prison. The barred windows let in the weak afternoon light. One of my shoes squeaks lightly as I stand up on the stage. My shoes are warm and comfortable, solid and without holes—but it wasn't always that way.

As a child in Paynestown, St. Elizabeth, in Jamaica, I had one pair of shoes that I kept wrapped in a cloth when I was at home. I'd walk, barefoot, down the road to the church. About halfway there, I'd take the shoes out of the cloth, wipe my feet and put the shoes on. About halfway home, I'd take the shoes off, carefully wipe them clean and wrap them back in the cloth. The rest of the time, I went barefoot.

We had a small farmhouse with no electricity or running water. My mother was an asthmatic and when she would have an attack, I would stay home from school to take care of her. On those days, she would tell me, "Sweetie, you can become anything you want to become. Only you can stop you."

I lost my mother when I was thirteen years old. To this day, I can hear her voice encouraging me. It is a musical voice inside my spirit, and as I connect to it, it is as though I am singing the most glorious song. I hear the melody in Mama's voice. And, as I connect my ambition to that melody in her voice, to the instructions she gave me when I was a little girl, they become a song.

"Girl, you can be whatever you want to be. Nobody can stop you, no matter what."

Those words that Mama gave me before she died were the lyrics. My determination to continue despite any obstacle became the instruments. Each obstacle on my journey to this day, I see as a different instrument. I didn't see obstacles as negatives. I saw them as lessons. Each lesson added an instrument that only added to the song I was singing. Each obstacle only makes my song that much more beautiful.

I did not have the opportunity to go to high school; so, during the day I took nurses' training classes, and in the evening, I attended adult continuing education. While getting my nursing degree, I added many instruments to my song. I graduated and

I lost my mother when I was thirteen years old.

began nursing in the local hospital, still singing this song that I can become all that I want to become. Even while I was nursing, though, I felt a void inside of me. I did not know what was missing. But, I knew I loved to talk.

Then, I had the opportunity to work at the Jamaica Cultural Development Commission. I worked with people to identify their skills and talents and help put them into the Festival Exhibition. Let's say someone was a good cook—I would have that person create recipes and design a meal that would be entered into competition, with the potential for winning national recognition and publicity in the media. Slowly, the space in the void inside was filling. I was more satisfied with what I was doing.

I did not realize it at the time, but what I was doing was coaching people. It was not until I came to America that I learned about the term "coaching" and realized that what I had been doing my entire life was coaching people to become their best. And, I was still singing my song. I sang it to myself, and I sang it to the people I coached. "You can become anything you want to become. No one can stop you but you."

My song sustained me and gave me strength and hope through my own adversities and doubt. I could listen with my heart and hear my mother's melody in my head. "No one can stop you, no matter what."

Early in my marriage I had my first miscarriage. With the tears running down my face, I said, "I am going to be a mother. Maybe not this time, but I know that I will one day be a loving, caring mother."

After five miscarriages, five horrible obstacles, my son was born, happy and healthy. My song carried me through.

Years later, my son and I were homeless. It was a terrible obstacle, having nowhere to live. But, I knew that experience was temporary. I knew that, no matter what, we would not be at that place forever. I knew like I knew my name that I was going to be

"No one can stop you, no matter what."

okay, that we were going to be okay. I was shaking and alone, but I hugged my child and I hummed my song. I knew that we were going to be all right. And, we were. Again, my song carried me through.

We are often given more than we think we can bear. When my son was incarcerated, I found myself dealing with the foreclosure of my home. Rather than succumb to the stress of crisis, my song gave me the courage to keep on. During that difficult time, I chose to focus on my future. I attended college on Tuesday and Thursday evenings and all day on Saturdays and Sundays to get my degree.

Sometimes, you can sing your song loud and strong. Sometimes, you can barely whisper it. But it's always there, inside you. Your song will carry you through. My song is still carrying me. When people tell me that I can't do this and why don't I do that, I listen and I respect what they say, but I don't always accept it.

I've met obstacles in my career, too. One evening, I met a gentleman. He asked, "What is your profession?"

I told him, "I am a motivational speaker."

And he said, "Oh! You can't be a motivational speaker with that accent!"

I heard his words, but I held onto my song that I could be anything I want to be. I knew I could not speak with another accent. I could not give up the accent, the sound of my mother's voice. I would not give up the melody of my song. And, so I said to him, "Watch me."

When I was inaugurated as president of the National African American Speakers Association, I made sure to invite that gentleman. In my speech, I mentioned that a prominent gentleman in the field once told me that, with my accent, I could not be a motivational speaker. I asked, "I wonder where he is today?"

I am not in the business of embarrassing people, so I did not call his name. But, when I looked in his direction, I saw that he was one of the first to applaud.

**There is always your song
deep inside of you.**

My song has carried me from the farmlands of Jamaica to a global platform, and I am still using this voice with this accent to bring joy to people's lives, to help them reinvent their lives so they can authentically be the people they were created to be.

This is the message I share with my audience at the women's prison. Before I can get very far into my speech, a prisoner interrupts me, saying, "Can you give me a minute, ma'am? I just have to run downstairs."

I look at the correctional officer. He nods his permission and the woman quickly leaves. In a few moments, she comes back with ten more women. She'd gone down to the general population and told all of the women who were Jamaican, "Your countrywoman is upstairs speaking, and you need to come and listen."

So, with my Jamaican accent, with my mother's voice, with my song guiding me through, I tell these women what I know. As I speak and share my story of hope and inspiration, I see women using the hems of their sweatshirts to wipe their tears. When I finish, a long line of people comes up to talk to me and thank me for giving them hope.

There is still hope for you, too. There is always your song deep inside of you. You must tap into that force to not look outside of yourself, but to look inside and find the song that's always been there and embrace it. If people say, "Just forget about that," let it go. Don't you ever give up on your song, because that is your certainty. Your song is what propels you, what keeps you going. Believe, believe, believe in it and never let it go.

What do you hear during times of great stress or great joy? Is it a beloved remembered voice? Is it music that lifts your spirit? Is it your grandfather's voice encouraging you as he taught you to ride a bicycle as a child? Is it your aunt's bubbling laughter that has always made you laugh along too? Is it your best friend's words of comfort, reassuring you that life will go on?

What will you do, what will you become, when you listen to your song? What shoes might you be standing in a year from now if you let your song guide you?

Dr. Daphne Clarke-Hudson's presence goes way beyond a nationally recognized empowerment specialist and professional keynote presenter. She's also an insightful author with multiple accredited works, a vibrant, award-winning radio personality and a certified transformational coach. Building on more than twenty years' experience helping others create the lives they envision, Dr. Daphne brings a whole world of insight to any table.

Dr. Daphne is a warm, bright inspiration: a powerful visionary who guides today's leaders and empowers tomorrow's leaders to fulfill their life purposes with hope, enthusiasm and resilience, to live life empowered and never look back. Unlock your full potential at www. Blogtalkradio.com/Daphne-Clarke-Hudson and also connect with Dr. Daphne at www.DaphneClarkeHudsonEmpowers.com.

WINSTON GREEN, JR.

WAKE UP TO YOUR PURPOSE

From an early age, I knew that I wanted to excel, to be better than average. I had big dreams and any time I told my friends about those dreams they would say, "Win, you're crazy. That's only on TV."

My response was always the same: "Where do you think they get that from? Someone must be doing it." I always had the "why not me?" attitude—if someone is going to succeed, why not me?

At fifteen, I lied about my age so I could get a job at the Waffle House to save money for a car. I bought my first car at fifteen, before I could even drive it myself. I went on to be the youngest graduate in my high school class, setting my sights on becoming a doctor because they wore those black wingtip shoes. I worked hard and long hours to reach my goals.

My dream of becoming a doctor changed after a summer internship helped me realize I didn't like patient care. I decided to finish my degree in biology and work in a lab as a toxicologist, chemist and medical technician. It wasn't long before I burned out. I would see sales reps come into my office and think, "Man, it would be cool to have a job like that."

So, I accepted a position with a leading medical equipment company, where in four short years, I became one of their leading sales reps in the country.

Despite my success, I was laid off shortly thereafter. It was one of the scariest moments of my life. My wife was pregnant with our twins; she had been laid off from her position in the airline industry after 9/11; *and* we were building a house. I was traumatized. I worked so hard, achieved so much, and yet was still at the mercy of my employers. That day I made a vow: "I will never work in a corporate job again. I will not let anyone control my time or my destiny, again."

I had been dabbling in real estate before being let go from my job, and I decided this was just the push I needed to go full force. When I came home and told my wife about my plans, she looked at me as if I was crazy. But I was used to people thinking I was crazy. I took my "why not me" attitude and pushed forward, turning down headhunter after headhunter with corporate job offers.

Keeping my head up and my eyes on the prize, I found a mentor who offered to show me the business. For the next year, I did nothing but learn about the real estate industry. I opened my own office and, working day and night, built it into a resounding

If someone is going to succeed, why not me?

success. My wife was able to stay home with the kids. We hired a live-in nanny to make her life easier, put the kids in private school and set about creating a life that looked very much like the one in my dreams.

Along the way, I tried to help anyone and everyone to rise above their circumstances and reach their full potential. I figured with my "why not attitude," my experience and my knowledge, I could help even the most challenged souls find their way and achieve success. So, I pushed the people I loved. I hired many family members and even paid their bills so they could be free from that anxiety and focus on work. I thought I knew best; I thought I could save people, fix people, help them realize their dreams.

My own dreams just got bigger. In 2005, I saw the real estate market changing and decided to change with it, venturing into residential development. By 2007, I had developed a multi-million dollar property. I sacrificed time with my family, missing school and sporting events, but I knew that my efforts would provide them with security and comfort. I thought I was doing the right thing. I thought it was worth it.

Then, just before the real estate market crashed, I lost the property. I will never forget the day I had to look into the faces of my investors, my wife and my family and break the news to them. I owned a fifteen million-dollar property but I didn't have fifteen dollars in my pocket.

I fought to keep the property, and I was still fighting when my wife sat me down to tell me she wanted out.

It was time to redefine my idea of success.

"I'm not in love with you anymore."

The day before Thanksgiving in 2008, my wife of ten years sat me down to tell me she was throwing in the towel. I was in shock. We had a good life—or a life that most people would consider a good life: three beautiful children, a nice house and, up until the year before, conveniences and privileges provided by my successful real estate business.

That day, my wife didn't attend Thanksgiving dinner at my parents' house as planned. I made it through the day on autopilot, memories of what brought me to this point flashing through my mind.

Dumbfounded and scared, I went to church to seek answers. I was starting to see that, in my pursuit of financial freedom, I hadn't spent enough time with my children or my wife. I had prioritized success and wealth over nurturing my most important relationships.

At church, I shared with my friend Eddie what happened, and he advised, "Go home and fight for your marriage. Don't give up."

I told my wife, "I didn't realize it at the time, but I finally get it. I'm sorry. I'll do anything. I'll do whatever it takes."

She looked at me and said, "I've been gone for five years. Why did it take you so long to notice?"

I begged her to work on our marriage, to go to counseling with me, to reconsider, but she had already made up her mind. Still, I tried. Even when she moved out of the house in May of the following year, I still held out hope that we would be able to repair the damage and reconcile. The day she moved out, I sat in the house and watched her gather her things. She was moving small items; she didn't take any furniture.

I said, "I hope you don't mind that I'm not helping you."

She understood. I just couldn't do it. As the door shut behind her I put my head in my hands and thought, "What on earth do I do now?"

I never want to relive that year; it was a very hard and dark time. I believed I had failed in business, and failed in my personal life. Wasn't I the one who made anything happen? Wasn't I the

Money is just a small aspect of life.

one who saved people? Wasn't I the one who did the impossible? I was devastated. "Lord, give me the strength and courage to get through this," I prayed.

Over the next two years, I sought my next business venture while simultaneously attempting to find myself. I asked myself, "What do you want to do next? What do you want your life to look like? How can you work less and still live your dreams?" It was time to redefine my idea of success.

I partnered with a friend to open my financial firm in 2011. I worked diligently to build my practice, studying and trying to learn the industry while working feverishly to meet the right types of clients—all while maintaining a more balanced life. When you are broke and desperate, it's a bit challenging to attract people with money, and unfortunately, those were the types of people that I needed to meet. I prayed to God for direction and understanding of my situation, and finally He answered my prayers when I closed my first business transaction. That allowed me to catch up on some extremely past-due bills, to collect my thoughts and eventually see a little light over the horizon.

I continued to educate myself in the industry and changed my environment in an effort to surround myself with the types of individuals that could get me the success that I needed.

This time, however, it wasn't just about big dreams of financial success. I surrounded myself with positive people. I opened myself to new ideas and to healing. I read books, and exercised and delved

On the other side of that sadness is growth.

further into myself and my spirituality. I continued to work to reconcile with my wife, convinced that if I could just redirect my focus, I could get her back.

During a run one day I heard Sting's song, "If You Love Somebody Set Them Free" and realized I was pushing for something that my wife didn't want.

When I got home I called her and asked, "On a scale of one to ten, how badly do you want this divorce?"

"Twelve," she replied.

"Okay," I said. "I won't fight you on this anymore. You can have the divorce."

There was nothing else I could do. I had done everything in my power to save our marriage, but it had died long before I realized my wife was in pain. It was time for me to focus on myself. For years I had assumed that my purpose was financial freedom—but what if it wasn't? What if I had been so consumed by ego and the drive to succeed that I had left no room for my true purpose?

It wasn't until my fall from grace that I realized what was important. I know now that God puts certain situations in our paths to help us grow. However, most of us do not realize it. The faster we can get over the anger, resentment and negative emotions and accept where we are on our journeys, the faster we can discover our true purposes. For me, that purpose is living a balanced life. It doesn't mean giving up on financial freedom; it just means I live a well-rounded life in pursuit of that goal.

Today, I never miss a soccer game or dance recital. My ex-wife and I have a beautiful co-parenting relationship, sharing custody and responsibilities. I still remember the day she left as if it was yesterday; that was the day I determined I would become a well-balanced man: spiritually, physically, mentally, emotionally and financially.

I had to be humbled to realize that money is just a small aspect of life. No amount of money or acclaim is worth more than my children saying, "Dad, did you see that goal?" or "Dad, did you see that performance?"

I tell people all the time, "I'd go through all of these experiences again just to have the relationship I have with my children today."

Beyond achieving balance and being present for my children, the financial and personal failures I experienced that terrible year paved the way to a new understanding about myself that I could not have come to otherwise. I met a wonderful woman who helped me see that I had been personalizing nearly everything in my life—if something went wrong, or right; if someone succeeded or failed; if people I loved were happy, sad, angry, scared or beaten down, I either felt responsible for the problem or felt I was the only one who could save the day.

Acknowledging all of the ways I personalized my successes and failures, and those of others close to me, helped me to let go of that personalization. It's so freeing to take yourself out of the equation, and to recognize that you're not the cause, or the cure. When you do all you can and you still end up coming up short, that's just life. When someone chooses to ignore your advice or to follow a different path than the one you imagine for them, that's just life.

Letting go of personalization is the true freedom. Seeing this enabled me to move past my failures and ensure that I was not defined by them.

I now have a successful financial services firm that allows me the privilege to educate individuals on financial strategies that can change their lives for generations to come. I have a wonderful relationship with my children and a beautiful partner and I am at peace while I venture on this journey called life.

So often, when we fail, we let the devastation eat us up inside, missing out on the true opportunity of the fall. Losing something dear to us is sad, of course, but on the other side of that sadness is growth. The gift of loss or failure is the ability to strip down to what is essential, free from expectation. When you fall down, you have a chance to see the world—and yourself—from a different perspective. There, on the ground, you can look up and see a purpose you may not have realized if you hadn't fallen. There, on the ground, you can look up and see a future you didn't know was possible!

Winston Green, Jr., is dedicated to empowering and educating individuals in an effort to eradicate financial illiteracy. He takes a unique approach to teach his clients the best practices that achieve wealth and financial security.

Winston is a graduate of Oakwood University, where he majored in biology and chemistry. He is a chemist, medical technologist and toxicologist who had the privilege to work with major medical firms in the area of medical equipment sales.

He has also had a successful and extensive background in the financial services arena for the last fifteen years. He was a former real estate investor, builder and developer in the Greater Atlanta area. Winston has used real estate to empower individuals in his community to understand and appreciate home ownership and getting a piece of the "American dream." Winston decided to apply that experience and coupled it with cutting-edge financial strategies to create an organization that focuses on principles that help his clients achieve attainable and rewarding financial goals.

Winston is extremely passionate and dedicated to exposing these concepts to all of his clients in an effort to shift the average mindset, to create generational wealth and to assist his clients in leaving a legacy. His commitment is to offer sound financial solutions: "It is not enough for us to do what we do best; our clients are top priority, we help them achieve what they do best." Connect with Winston at www. SovFinancial.com.

MICHAEL LIFSHITZ

CLIMBING YOUR STAIRS TO SUCCESS

W e've all heard inspirational stories of people who have hit rock bottom—those who have had a defining moment of astronomical pain or heartache and ultimately rose from that challenge. More often than not, most of us won't have one point in time that defines us in such a way, either by our challenges or our successes.

Many of us have regular day-to-day challenges, some visible, some hidden. Many of us have various limitations blocking us from reaching our full potential, either by circumstance or possibly by our own doing. So, the first question is: What's blocking us? What's keeping us from realizing the dreams and goals we hope to achieve?

Several years ago, I was invited to a networking meeting. I hadn't been to this particular location before, so I didn't know what to expect. I arrived, and as I got out of my car and approached the entrance, I stopped in my tracks. In front of me was a staircase. It had no railing. It's just a staircase, right? Just five steps to climb, and you're finished with it. Most people don't even think about stairs; they just automatically climb them, their minds running with their daily plans or maybe carrying on a conversation with a colleague or friend.

They're just stairs.

I was born with a condition called Multiple Congenital Musculoskeletal Abnormalities. During my childhood, I had eight operations and then a ninth when I hit my teens. I wear a prosthetic leg and use a cane, but for long-distances, I have a wheelchair.

I can use stairs, albeit not as swiftly as others. There is a caveat: The stairs need to have a railing.

As I stood at the base of this insurmountable obstacle trying to figure out what to do, I looked around for a ramp, anything to help me out of this situation. Nothing. However, I noticed that a piece of paper had been taped to one of the entrance doors. I asked someone passing by what it said, and it turned out that my meeting had been relocated.

They were just stairs. And, fortunately, I didn't need to climb them that day. Sometimes, what's blocking us is easily identified and conquered. Sometimes, we can easily walk away. Sometimes, meetings get moved to places that are wheelchair accessible. And sometimes, there are stairs with no railings in buildings with no visible ramp or elevator.

That doesn't mean there isn't a solution, though. It just means we have to figure a way around those stairs. We all face challenges; the question is will we let them stand in our way or find a way around them to achieve our goals.

The first question is: What's blocking us?

In 2006, I lost a bet I made with my friend. Fortunately, he lost it, too, and had to participate in the "punishment" with me. That was one of the best losses of my life. On January 27, 2006, I stepped on stage for a comedy open mic night. I loved it. Performing comedy opened up a whole new world for me. I learned just how powerful humor can be, how it can connect us, sensitize us to one another and help us look at the bad things in our lives in a far more positive way.

The more I connected with my audiences, the more I realized that, while I was focusing on showing them what people with disabilities can do, another far more important point was being made. While my challenges are more apparent, we all face challenges. The only difference is that mine get me better parking spots. So, if we all face challenges, that means that we can all overcome challenges.

They're just stairs.

When I'm doing stand-up, I talk about how I don't really care for a lot of politically correct terminology, with the exception of the term "differently abled." That's a great descriptor. We're all differently abled in that we all have our own way of doing things. I

You can be a victim, or you can be a victor.

can get from point A to Z same as anyone, but my method is a little flashier with my wheelchair. The important part is that we are all capable of ending up at the same place. We are all able to overcome whatever challenge we're faced with in order to get to point Z; we just might have to get there in different ways.

The point is to do it. Find a way to do it. Now, funny enough, I was invited to another meeting at that same building with the railless staircase. This time, however, when I got out of the car and remembered, "Oh, right. Stairs," I paused, let myself think, and wondered if maybe there was another way around this. I got into my car, drove around to the back, and lo and behold there in the back of the building was disabled parking, a ramp to get inside and an elevator to the restaurant where my event was being held.

You can be a victim, or you can be a victor. A victim is stuck, mired down by everything that has gone wrong. A victim is trapped by the thought, "I can't." A victor is someone who has figured out what's blocking them and blasted through it. A victor is someone who knows that it may not be easy, but that it can be done. A victor is someone who told themselves, "Sure I can."

Don't accept people's definition of who you are. Don't accept the limitations that people may put on you. You are in charge of what you can do. You decide who you will be. As my condition progressed, I realized that I would have to move from using a cane to an electronic chair and I didn't like that idea. I fought getting one for a few years, in fact. Boy, should I have gotten that chair sooner than I did! I can go farther and, in some ways, accomplish more than I did before.

I'd told myself that I needed to prove to people that I could manage with only a cane. I was making myself work harder than necessary. It turned out that my chair was like that sign on the door telling me that I didn't need to work so hard after all. Sometimes we block ourselves, because we're not seeing a different way to accomplish the same thing.

Now I realize that when people see that chair they assume I can do less. I don't let that affect me. I know exactly what I'm capable of and, more importantly, how well I can do it. I've simply added a tool to my life that affords me more opportunities than before. There will always be those who don't see it that way. The difference is that I don't let their mindset stop me. I don't let their definition of who I am affect how I see myself or what I believe I can accomplish. I don't let them block me from getting where I want to go.

I know myself better than they do, after all. They're just stairs.

Challenge your own perception of what you're able to do. In 2009, I participated in a fundraiser for Easter Seals that involved me rappelling off a building. Some folks might see that as crazy. I don't necessarily have the strength in my limbs to properly maneuver. It would have been easy to skip out on participating because of my condition. But I didn't let that stop me and I did it. Now admittedly, as you stand on the ledge of the building three hundred and eighty feet in the air and someone tells you lean back, the rope will hold you, there is a strong urge to back out. However, had I backed out, I would have missed out on the exhilarating feeling as I arrived at the bottom to the cheers of people watching and the same sense of pride I feel to this day when I watch the video of me doing the rappel.

A new doctor was assigned to me when I was eighteen. This guy had the personality of wet paint. As we went through the initial consultation, I mentioned that after the appointment I was going back to school. This surprised him, as if something that was wrong with my feet meant that there was something wrong with my brain. Well, I graduated with honors and got into an exclusive co-op program at university, so it's safe to say that his expectations of what I could achieve were grossly underestimated.

If I listened to everyone who told me that my disability meant I wouldn't be able to do anything, I'd be at home, jobless and depressed.

It's not about proving people wrong or doing something simply because someone told you that you can't. That's not going to make you happy in the long run. There are always going to be people who can only see the negative in your life. It's about doing something

It's all about a plan of persistence.

you want to do, doing things you love, living the life you want for yourself. Don't be the obstacle that holds your future happiness back. Take action.

So I ask you: What are your stairs?

If you had no obstacle in your life and could do what you truly wanted, what would that be? Why aren't you doing that? What's keeping you from that? How are you going to deal with those stairs? Or hey, is there a sign somewhere telling you that you don't even need to deal with those stairs, that you could walk away? Whatever it is you want for yourself in life, find a way. Do not give up. Go behind the building and look for that alternate entrance.

While it's true we may not all have the financial freedom to just up and change careers, if you hate your current job and wish you could do something else, the question you should ask yourself is, "What will make me happier?" It may not happen straight away, but if you keep plugging away at that goal, you'll eventually get there. It's all about a plan of persistence.

That's not to say that it's going to come easy. That's why success feels so good when you achieve it. You put that work in, be it studying hard, going for the job you've always wanted or putting your neck out to try something new. You persevere; you find a way around your obstacles; you meet those challenges. You keep moving forward.

I have it relatively easy in comparison to other folks. I have a wheelchair and I have self-confidence. Both of those tools help me in my life tremendously. As Robert F. Kennedy paraphrased George Bernard Shaw, "There are those that look at things the way they are, and ask *why*? I dream of things that never were, and ask *why not*?"

Why not? Why not you? That's the question to ask yourself: Why not? Why not you? We all face challenges in life, every one of us. There's no reason why you can't be one of those exceptional people who looks at those challenges dead on and comes up with a solution, who climbs to the top.

Go over. Go under. Go around or go through. But never give up on your dreams.

Michael Lifshitz, born and raised in Montreal with a condition called Multiple Congenital Musculoskeletal Abnormalities, not only earned his MBA from Edinburgh Business School, but also became a chartered professional accountant, started and sold his own accounting and financial planning practices and continued a successful career in finance and accounting. Michael uses motivational speaking, comedy and writing to enlighten and inspire people as to what people with disabilities can accomplish. Connect with Michael at www. MichaelLifshitz.com.

PAUL DIXON

HONORING PAPA LEMON AND MAMA SARAH

"So… What do you think?"

My former wife and I were sitting in my cousin Lehman's house one August afternoon in 2003, and he had just told us all about the book he had been writing about our grandparents, Papa Lemon and Mama Sarah. Living in Minnesota, I only saw them once a year during their summer visit from their home in Mississippi, so I never really knew them. But, Lehman did, and he had taken their personalities and life lessons he had been taught and turned them into characters for a series of fun and educational children's books.

What did I think? I thought it was a fantastic idea. But, as I sat across from Lehman, I thought, *This is an interesting opportunity, but I'm just not ready to be involved at this time.*

I was born in Minneapolis, and have lived in the Twin Cities my entire life. I was raised by my mother in a single-parent household along with my older sister, and I guess you could say that we were economically disadvantaged. The city bus was our main source of transportation; food stamps, free school lunch and rent subsidies were all just a part of life. Despite all this, education was always the key factor. In 1982 I was the class valedictorian at Minneapolis South High School and in 1986 I graduated with a business degree from the University of Minnesota Carlson School of Management.

I never worry about the "how," because life unfolds for me exactly as it should. While looking for work after graduation, someone I had gone to school with but barely knew called me and said, "I have a friend who's a recruiter, and they're looking for people for entry-level positions at Target."

I went for it, even though I hadn't even been looking at Target. I worked in merchandising in a variety of areas, culminating with working as a senior buyer in toys for five years.

The opportunity to work on this project with Lehman came at exactly the right time because after working for the company for sixteen years, the time came for me to move on. I resigned in December 2002, with no idea of what my next career move would entail. During the following year, I had a variety of toy consulting projects, but nothing really seemed to stick. I turned to my faith, asking, "What am I supposed to do? How am I supposed to do it?"

And, the answer came: "Let your faith guide you. Don't worry about how things are going to go."

One day in the spring of 2003, I was shopping at Target and happened to run into my cousin Sabrina, Lehman's sister. I was a shy person by nature, and my first instinct was not to say anything, but something told me, *you should say hello to her.*

We made the usual small talk, and after a while, she said, "Paul, I have to show you this article. Our grandmother, Mama Sarah, just had her hundredth birthday celebration!"

Let your faith guide you.

I didn't even realize that Mama Sarah was one hundred. I gave her my business card so that she could send me the article, and a few months later, for the first time in his life, Lehman called me.

"I have a business idea that I'd like to show you," Lehman said, and we met soon after. Following that first meeting in 2003, when I had initially thought that it wasn't the right time for me to get involved, we had various other meetings throughout 2004, and I felt more and more compelled to be a part of it. I read the first manuscript and I could see it as a fun and fascinating concept on its own, but the fact that my grandparents were the main characters made me sit back and think, *This is a really cool story.*

As we talked more, however, I discovered so much that I never knew about my grandparents. I learned that Papa Lemon was a man who was really well-loved by his community.

Lehman was in awe of him, and he told me, "Papa Lemon made me feel like the most important child in the world. He had that personality that could really connect."

We've been spiritually guided along the way.

I had no idea that our grandfather was so admired by so many people. I remembered Mama Sarah her being a soft-spoken and beautiful woman: peaceful, kind and open to everyone.

"She's an angel," Lehman told me.

I was sold, and in July 2004, we officially formed our business and published the first Papa Lemon book. When we picked up the first batch and opened the box, I held a copy in my hands and thought, *This is so surreal. A year ago, Lehman and I were virtually strangers, and here we are.*

The project was so far from what I expected to do with my life—I was a corporate guy; I never had any inclination to get involved in a small entrepreneurial venture—but it was as if all the ducks just lined up in a row for us. Who was I to be worrying about the *how* when things had come together so wonderfully? I couldn't find it in myself to worry, because with such strong circumstances, where was the risk?

The first out-of-state event that we attended to promote "The Adventures of Papa Lemon's Little Wanderers" series of books was the June 2006 Frasernet conference in Atlanta. This was the beginning of connecting with others across the country and sharing the Papa Lemon books. One year later, I was sitting at our exhibition table at an event in the Twin Cities when a young boy around ten or eleven years old came and bought one of the books. He was quite shy, and I remembered him because I'd always had similar problems myself.

The boy came back about thirty minutes later, approached the table and said, "I just wanted to let you know that I finished the book and I really, really enjoyed it. Could I buy the other ones?"

It was an affirming moment, and while I had always had faith in the project, this was something different. This was someone who had never heard of my grandparents and was moved by the very idea of them.

Later that year at an event in downtown Minneapolis in the middle of October, I was sitting at my table with the books when a gentleman in his late thirties or early forties happened by. He glanced up at the Papa Lemon sign on my table and kept walking, but all of a sudden he stopped and turned around to come back to the table.

He pointed up at the sign and said, "Hey, I know Papa Lemon! I was in jail when I read that book, and I have no idea how I got it, but it was a really good read, and it helped me through the place I was in at that time."

I was touched and even more convinced that my faith was steering me in the right direction.

While I hadn't just been sitting back waiting for things to happen, I had never had any kind of game plan set in stone, yet here was a crystal clear sign that I had made the right choice in being a part of the project. I had made the right choice in not worrying about the how. To know that the reach of the story extended beyond mere historical fiction adventures and could help grown adults through troubling times made me think, *This is really something.* And, just like that, the Papa Lemon concept grew bigger than either of us.

It's never been "here's the plan;" rather, we've been spiritually guided along the way. The only reason we went to Frasernet back in 2006 was that I had seen an advertisement, and it just kind of hit me: *We're supposed to go.* There have been too many other similar experiences for it to all be coincidence. It definitely hasn't been a straight-line path to get to where we are today, but no one has a crystal ball—patience, persistence and faith in our project have seen us through.

The biggest lesson both Lehman and I have learnt throughout this journey we are taking with Papa Lemon and Mama Sarah is that we can't be concerned with the how. We both answered a call, and when that kind of faith is instilled, it becomes unnecessary to concern yourself with the details of the journey—it's the destination that's important.

It's about reaching those life-affirming moments, like when just a month before her death, Mama Sarah was able to see and hold a copy of the very first published Papa Lemon book. I believed

**You have to trust that you will
never be steered wrong.**

Mama Sarah actually touching the book was a spiritual sign that she blessed and approved what Lehman and I were doing. Those moments reinforce my faith and my belief in my path and this project.

Having faith in what you're doing ultimately means that there is no risk. Even if something has gone badly, you have to trust that you will never be steered wrong.

If I hadn't resigned from my job and wound up looking for a new direction, I would never have considered my partnership with Lehman a viable option, since I just wouldn't have had the time or energy to devote to it. But, it is because of this project that I have shifted into a different person, with a greater understanding of people and of myself.

Sometimes we just look at the names on a family tree, but we don't think about the people behind those names, their inherent qualities and the choices they made that have influenced us and who we are today. When you understand your grandparents and other ancestors, you understand yourself. What could you come to know about yourself if you explored the history of the people who planted your roots? And, what could you achieve if you answered your own call and stopped worrying about the how?

There are so many ways to honor a legacy—what way would you choose?

Paul Dixon has over twenty years' experience in the toy industry and currently works in sales for Disney Consumer Products. He co-founded the Matter of Africa America Time Corp. in order to publish The Adventures of Papa Lemon's Little Wanderers *book series. To learn more about the books and to connect with Paul, visit www. PapaLemonEDU.com.*

STACEY MOLLISON

A FAILED SUICIDE SAVED MY LIFE

I'm still alive, I thought, taking in the sterile surroundings of my hospital room. My mother sat by my bedside with her eyes rimmed in red and my stepfather was pacing the floor, both with matching expressions of worry and fear, though I knew instantly that what they were afraid of wasn't that I was in the hospital to begin with—it was that I would reveal to the authorities *why* I was in the hospital at all.

I was sixteen years old and I was lying in that hospital bed because I had attempted suicide. Everything seemed so fuzzy as I tried to remember what got me to this point.

My parents had held a function at our house, and I accepted a ride to the mall with the nephew of my stepfather's friend who was at their party. When I came back home everything seemed out of control.

My stepfather yelled, "You should have known better!"

Before I could ask questions or give explanations he started beating me with the hose from the washing machine. During the confusion, I learned that the guy had stolen one of our television sets.

How the heck was I to know that someone you invited to our home was a thief, and I shouldn't have taken a ride with him? I wondered.

It was his brother who pulled my stepfather off of me as my mother and the rest of the guests stood watching, telling him, "Come on, man. You can't do this to her."

His brother lifted me off the ground and carried me to my room, where I was left, trembling and weak, remembering all of the other times this had happened and deciding: This is the last time. I lay on my bed, hands shaking uncontrollably, and thought, *No one loves me. I'm not safe here. I'm so tired.*

My stepfather and I had such a volatile relationship that I slept with a knife under my pillow. I took out the knife and weighed it in my hands for a moment, anger and desperation rising up inside me like a tidal wave as I contemplated ways to put an end to my suffering. *Death,* I thought. It seemed almost immediately clear

It seemed I had become my mother.

to me, and as that wave of desperation crested, I tore across my room and stabbed the word "Death" into the bottom of my door. Seeing the word so crudely carved into the wood strengthened my resolve, and I went to the bathroom, wrenched open the medicine cabinet and started taking pills.

As I woke up in that hospital room, disoriented, fuzzy memories of how I got there rushed to the surface—trying to come down the stairs and falling; my sister, screaming as she found me at the bottom. There was and still is a gap between that last memory and waking up in the hospital and being grateful that I'm still alive. I'm still here.

My mother and stepfather were talking in low voices, but I couldn't hear their conversation over the voices in my own head: *I'm glad I'm still alive. I promise myself I will never allow him or anyone else to make me feel that worthless again. I can't believe that I allowed him to make me do that. This cannot happen again. I'm happy I'm still alive and I'm not going to let him get to me.*

When I got home, there was no change in my parents' behavior. There was, however, a change in me. This time, I was fueled to change my situation by an entirely different kind of determination. I stayed out of the house a lot more, spending time with my friends and my grandmother and trying to add more hours at my job. But I would never leave entirely because I believed that my mother needed someone there to help protect her from him. A piece of me never forgot listening for my mother's screams at night during yet another fight between her and my stepfather. Even though nothing changed, I no longer had the same level of despair. I told myself: *If I never get the love from others I wanted, it doesn't matter, because I'm responsible for loving me.*

The years slowly crept by and little changed at home. I started dating and I was still living at home when I became pregnant at twenty-one, in my senior year in college. The day my son was born

I would forever be caught in this cycle.

and I held him in my arms, I knew I would never return to that house and put my child in harm's way. I went straight from the hospital to my grandmother's house and never went back to live at that house again.

When my son was five months old, I was savagely assaulted by his father. I was fully committed to not living my mother's life until that day it seemed I had become my mother.

That afternoon my son's father had dropped me off at the hairdresser, and when he showed up early at the salon, I looked up at him and said, "Hey, you're early. I didn't call you yet; we're not quite finished."

He didn't even respond, simply walked up to me and started beating the living daylights out of me in front of the hairdresser, who was the only other person there.

"What happened?" I screamed at him over and over, trying desperately to understand.

This can't be happening, I thought. *This is not my life.* Though we had had violent verbal altercations, he had never hit me. I had no idea what was going on.

My hairdresser screamed, "I'm calling the police!" When I briefly managed to get away from him and into the small kitchenette at the back of the salon, blood pouring from my mouth, I flashed on the knife my sixteen-year-old self had kept under her pillow and started yelling at the girl to get one.

As soon as she said, "The police are on their way," my son's father dragged me out of there, threw me in the car and sped off with me.

Desperate to get away, I kept frantically wrenching the steering wheel and turning us into oncoming traffic, shouting at him, "We're both going to die! Our son is going to be without both parents!"

Time after time he shook me off, until he couldn't anymore; he pulled over and I jumped out and called my brother, who came and picked me up. When I got back to my grandmother's house,

**I began to understand what a balanced
life should look and feel like.**

I learned that my son's father answered the phone; it was an ex-boyfriend and they got into a verbal altercation. My son's father got angry and decided to take his anger out on me.

The next day, I was scheduled to go to Atlanta for a job interview, and I traveled there battered black and blue. Every moment I was away, I kept thinking: *Do you want to continue this and be a victim like your mother, or do you want to change this for you and your child?* I promised myself I would never go back to the abuse and danger of my parents' home after my son was born—how could I justify returning to an identical situation now? I realized that my life was dangerously out of balance and I ran.

I went to Atlanta with little money and no car, to sleep on a mattress on the floor of a one-bedroom apartment. After I settled in, it was as if a dam inside me shattered; I spent long days alone and crying, dealing with the realization that, emotionally, I didn't have it together. Having been in survival mode for so long while I helped my mother, finished school and had my baby, I didn't know how else to be—I was still incredibly high-strung, volatile and argumentative.

One day, my mother called me from New York, frenzied and crying after yet another altercation with my stepfather. Immediately, I called a friend in New York.

"I need you to dial 911 for my mother," I told her. "He did it again."

I was nearly nine hundred miles away in Georgia and what was I doing? I was letting the guilt over not being near enough to help my mother send my savior complex into overdrive. Before I left New York, I decided to break away from abusive relationships. I thought I had left this all behind me. In that moment, I knew: "I can't outrun *me* just by changing location."

There had to be a commitment to do the work necessary to invite real change into my world, and I was the only one who could make that commitment. I had to make a decision about how I was

We all deserve to live the best life we can.

going to deal with this part of my life, otherwise I would forever be caught in this cycle.

When I was a sixteen-year-old girl, waking up in that hospital bed, I was given one more day. I'd known that I was going to have to do the work to keep that little glimpse of me that I saw and liked, and I hadn't been doing it.

The decision I made was to attend intensive therapy twice a week, one session on my own and the other as part of a group. One of the most important things that came out of it was: *I am more important than my mother, I have to place value on my own life, I cannot save her*—she *is responsible for her own life. I have to get rid of the guilt and the savior complex.* For the first time, I believed I'd done right by my sixteen-year-old self.

As I started to change who I was and restructure my life, I noticed how happy and free I felt and I began to understand what a balanced life should look and feel like. The most important part of healing was forgiving people for their behavior and making peace with what happened. I had to learn that I couldn't let my past define my present and my future and I had to make the tough decision of setting boundaries and deciding what type of relationships I *would* have.

Trying to talk about the abuse with my family was futile, and for years they did not want to discuss it. I was eventually able to talk with my mother and stepfather about that dark time in our lives, and they both apologized for what happened. I discovered that my stepfather was himself a victim of severe physical abuse by his mother. Even though the memories never go away, therapy helped me to find more effective ways of managing my life and changing negative messages and maladaptive behaviors.

During my introspective journey I began to realize there are three core areas of a balanced life: psychological and spiritual calmness, physical health and wellness and financial stability. Because I felt out of control and powerless, my life unfolded as it did. Having all three of the core areas consistently out of balance finally caused me to pay attention to how I was functioning and what I needed to do to live the life I wanted.

The failed suicide helped me to live my life with purpose and take responsibility for my destiny. I became focused and determined to be an improved version of myself. Success is not just about financial achievement but more about working through what some may consider failures and turning them into opportunities for growth. I have gained strength and a higher level of self-worth by no longer being a victim of my past circumstances. I now own an expanding business and have leveraged lessons learned to create more effective personal and professional relationships. My determination is that the cycle of violence ends with me.

We all deserve to live the best life we can. When loving ourselves becomes more important than anything or anyone else in our lives, we have the strength to make better decisions.

By deciding who and what has priority in our lives we regain the confidence, power, and control to manage our lives more effectively. Once we are able to finally put ourselves first and work to ensure consistent balance psychologically, physically and financially, we can maximize our potential for success.

Stacey Mollison is the founder of Libra Balancing Center (LBC), a center for change dedicated to creating a strategy for success by focusing on maintaining a balanced lifestyle. She developed the concept of the "3-Dimensional You," a program that teaches business professionals how to maximize their potential for success through creating consistent balance in three core areas: 1. psychological/spiritual calmness; 2. physical health and wellness; and 3. financial stability. She is also a trainer of the DISC Personality Profile and provides workshops nationally.

Stacey is the president and CEO of Libra Management Group, an SBA 8(a) Certified minority-woman-owned small business providing services in real estate, business management and consulting, event management, transportation and facilities support services. The firm is located in the Metro Atlanta area. She manages the operations of the firm to include: training, maintaining client relationships and developing new business opportunities.

In 2010 Stacey was named one of Atlanta's 50 Rising Stars by Atlanta Business Journal *and in 2014 the Atlanta Business League honored her as one of Atlanta's Top 100 Women of Influence.*

Stacey earned her BA in criminal justice & law from John Jay College, New York, her MA in psychology and professional counseling from Argosy University, Atlanta and a post-graduate certificate in marriage and family therapy from Argosy University, Atlanta. In 2011 she became a Certified Human Behavior Consultant and an Accredited DISC Training Provider. She is the 2014 president of the Empire Board of Realtists, Inc. in Atlanta, a local chapter of the National Association of Real Estate Brokers, Inc. (NAREB). She currently serves as the national secretary of NAREB's board of directors.

Stacey Mollison was born in Guyana, South America, migrated to the United States at age eleven and grew up in Brooklyn, NY until she moved to Atlanta in 1995 after completing her undergraduate work. She has two children a son (twenty) and daughter (thirteen).

Using her background in psychology, she believes in a holistic approach to creating an effective work-life balance. Start finding your own balance at www.LibraBalancingCenter.com.

ROSETTA WALKER

STEP INTO A NEW YOU

I was hospitalized and in a coma because of a head injury at two-and-a-half years of age. My doctor did not think I was going to live. I pulled through that near-death trauma by divine purpose. I am here to share some of my life's story with you.

When I was ten years old, my family began to attend church regularly. Being in that building gave me a feeling nothing else had in my short-yet-already-tumultuous life. Within those walls, surrounded by those wonderful people, my heart was lifted up by the beautiful hymns the choir sang; that was the moment when I felt real love.

This may not surprise many of you. After all, church is meant to be about surrounding yourself with God's unconditional love. However, until then, I had lived a life of fear, ridicule and shame. Because of sexual abuse at far too young an age, I was shy, withdrawn, dyslexic and barely able to speak without an embarrassing stammer, so I often *didn't* speak.

One day at home, I pulled out a spiral notebook, the kind that children used for school, and I began to write a song. I'd never written a song before, but something in me needed to get out. I titled it "Tell Me More about the Lord." This was so immense for me, truly life-changing. It was because I *finally* found a way to use my voice.

When I was very young, I suffered horrific sexual and physical abuse, leaving my body damaged and my spirit broken. As so often happens with small children who suffer in such a way, I internalized my pain, feeling ashamed of myself, afraid of the world and unworthy of love. Who could love broken, little old me?

Inside the walls of my church, however, I found the courage to allow myself to be loved. I don't mean to make this about religion: It's not. It's about love for all people. It's about loving yourself and letting yourself *be* loved. It's about finding what it is inside you that will help you move past your own hurts and step into the person you are meant to be.

For me it was writing and singing, but maybe you paint, maybe you garden or have some other thing that makes you feel good about yourself.

When I let that inside of me, that feeling of unconditional love, then I was finally able to begin speaking about my hurts and my past through writing. When I'm writing, no one can bother me— I'm locked into my personal, private space where I can express, feel and release all of that ugliness that we so often carry around in our hearts. Writing took me outside of what I had experienced, calmed me, helped me find my own peace. Many times as I wrote I cried desperately, releasing the pain and hurt into my songs and poems.

I had to learn to love myself.

It would take a long time for me to be able to vocalize even just a part of what had happened in my past, but when I put pen to paper, I didn't hold back. I allowed myself to feel all the emotions I'd tried to keep buried. I allowed myself to cry, to rage and finally to let go of the idea that I was a failure. It allowed me to heal.

I had to learn to love myself. When you keep your hurts buried inside, you deny yourself the opportunity and blessing of moving toward a life of peace and joy.

I continued to write songs and poetry as a teenager, letting those words help me move into the life I wanted. Sure, I made mistakes along the way, but I pushed myself harder to accomplish a goal that many people don't achieve until much later: At twenty-two I became ordained as a minister. This moment would change everything for me in the best of ways.

When I received my certification, right there on the paper was my full name, Rosetta Walker. That piece of paper didn't have the ugly nickname my siblings gave me, a name tied to my childhood trauma and the only name by which I had been known growing up. No, it was *me*. It was my name on that paper, who I really was. It said to me that I was someone worthy of love, worthy of accomplishment and worthy to help bring others along on their journey to fulfillment as well.

In time, I was able to let go of what was buried inside me. It didn't happen at all once. Writing poems, plays and music was a key element, but joining the ministry helped me tremendously, giving me a platform to spread the message that each and every

Each and every one of us is worthy of love.

one of us is worthy of love. Being able to focus on supporting others helped me to let go of what was inside of me, to pull out that rotten thorn that had festered, and instead fill myself up with things that were beautiful.

I've dedicated my life to finding the best way I can to empower, heal, love and encourage others to overcome their personal obstacles. Since setting myself free of my past—and writing this chapter, finally saying out loud what had happened to me is my way of letting that last piece go, so we are on this journey together!—I've been able to accomplish so much in my life.

No longer do I stammer or hide my voice, only letting my silent, hidden notebooks know how I feel. I've gone on to sing with amazing choirs around the world, have written and sung award-winning songs of inspiration, written books and published poems, was even nominated for Poet of the Year, and now I've been granted the opportunity to tell you this: You are worthy of love. Your background, the color of your skin or what you've been through doesn't matter.

You are worthy of love. As the Queen Of Inspiration I want to inspire and help you believe that. Just as I share with my fans, followers, friends and family, who are all known as my "LOVED ONES," I want to share with you these four steps that I truly believe can help you find your way back to loving yourself, to falling in love with your dreams once more and making them come true:

1. **Address:** Address your reality. It may be hurtful to go back and examine what has happened in your life. You must reject any negative thoughts that may come from making yourself remember. When you do this, you can no longer deny or drown out the truth of what has happened to you in your life. It's time to deal with it and stop blaming yourself. I encourage you to seek counseling or professional help if you can.

2. **Release:** Release all the pain and hurt you feel; cry if you need to. It's part of the healing process to free yourself. Have a friend or loved one assist you with this step, someone who understands, believes in and is supportive of you. This step is so important since many people who experienced abuse didn't have a support system in the first place. Release so you can get past the trauma, abuse, violence or anguish that plagues you. Clear your head of the past. Let go of all anger. This is *your* time for healing.

3. **Forgive:** This doesn't mean you will forget! But you must forgive whomever you believe caused the damage in your life even though you know they've wronged you. Forgive them so you can be free in your mind, heart and soul. Some things take longer than others to achieve, but you *can* be free of your past haunting you.

4. **Step Into:** Shake off the old you. You've earned the right. It's time to live a life of freedom and choice, of love and acceptance. It's time to step into a new *you!* Repeat to yourself until you believe it, "I have overcome the past in

my mind, heart and soul, and now I am victorious and free!"

Freedom is such an awesome thing to have. Reliving a painful past only holds you back from your dreams. I encourage you to make the decision to move forward today. Make the choice to change your life today. Don't let outside forces keep you from living your dream. I'm living this plan right now. Sharing this with you is the last shackle to my past, that final barrier, and it feels wonderful to let it go. Let go of what's buried inside so you can be free to become a better *you*, the person you were always meant to be.

Addressing and releasing the past helps us step into the fullness of our true human greatness. My first memory is one of the worst of my life. But I control the memories I make today, and they are filled with love and friendship, with humbling accomplishments and, most of all, with gratitude. That first sermon I gave as a newly ordained minister was a lesson from the book of Revelations. I had

Courage belongs to us all.

my own revelation at that moment: This would be my calling. I stepped up, not only to a pulpit, but into the person I was meant to become all along: someone with a message for all people, religious or not, that we need to share, to spread, to overwhelm one another with love.

Courage belongs to us all. We're quick to limit ourselves; we let challenges and negativity or our loved ones' lack of belief in our dreams and maybe even ourselves keep us from achieving them. Find the courage to love yourself and to love your dreams. But know that you have to not just have a dream, you have to *love* your dream and yourself unconditionally. That means that you will let *nothing* stop you from moving forward. You don't give up on things you love, right? So don't give up on yourself. Don't give up on your dream.

The tragedy is not what I went through. The tragedy would be my doing nothing about it!

It's time to turn your freedom light on; address, release, forgive and step into the life you were always meant to have. It's waiting for you!

Failure's Blessing

From the time of our birth
We enter into a new and sometimes strange earth
That we will have to get to know
As we learn and grow.
Some learn wisdom from making mistakes
And some from failures is what it takes.
Trials, tribulations, disappointments and all of life's lessons
Can turn into happiness and true blessings.
To go from being a child to a strong successful woman or man.
Here! In this moment you stand
To be able to boldly share failure's blessings in life hand in hand.

Multi-talented Rosetta Walker, bestselling author, singer, songwriter, poet, child activist, actress and radio host, is also the author of the book Love Is In The Air. *She has toured the globe, written songs and performed with renowned gospel choirs and singers, is a member of the Grammy-Award-voting Recording Academy and an ordained evangelist and a motivational speaker. She is the owner and CEO of Walker Records Production, RD Walker Publishing BMI and Rosetta Creations, Ltd. of which she is president. Her mission in life is to spread her message of love through all of her works. Connect with Rosetta at www.RosettaWalker.com. Her music is also available on iTunes: itunes. apple.com/ca/artist/rosetta-walker/id279257722.*

R. J. HODGES

BORN II WIN

Oftentimes, winning in life starts in a way that may resemble defeat. As a result of this, it is very important to understand that things are not always what they appear to be. The old adage, "looks can be deceiving" holds true in most of our lives. We have to develop vision beyond sight in order to truly understand the things that are working *for* us, as opposed to the things that seem to be working *against* us.

My introduction to what winning in life really means started late one Friday night about fifteen years ago. Nothing in my life was working the way I wanted it to, and defeat seemed more real than the hope that things would improve. I was having one of those pitiful moments, where negativity and feeling sorry for myself ruled.

Have you ever felt this way?

Let me give you the backstory that led to this point in time. I lost my father at the age of eight, grew up in a single parent household and watched my mother go through the struggles that come along with that. It wasn't easy, but she always figured out a way to provide for me, while instilling confidence that I could do and become anything I desired, no matter what.

In my late teenage years, my mother was diagnosed with cancer. This meant that I quickly had to convert from a youth simply trying to figure life out to a responsible man of the house. It was definitely not a situation I was prepared for. Nevertheless, my mother and I battled her illness together, truly giving that fight our all. However, shortly after my twentieth birthday, my mother passed away. There really are no words to describe my mental state at that point: the feeling of emptiness, isolation, or my dim outlook on what the future held.

My intent is not to tell a sob story about my life. Instead, it is an attempt to get you to consider how the difficult times of our lives, if viewed from the proper perspective, have played a role in our development. Take a moment to reflect on some of your own experiences. We all face life's challenges differently, and in the midst of the low moments it is very hard to see how they could ever serve us well.

Just a few years earlier, I was full of excitement and ambition. At eighteen years of age, I was fortunate enough to start my own business. Looking back, I was the definition of ignorance on fire. I truly knew nothing about business or how to handle the responsibilities that came along with that. The business suffered, not because it wasn't lucrative, but because I had not developed the inner characteristics required to create or sustain professional success. Often we want things in life that we are not equipped to handle yet and we get upset when those things don't materialize. We should be thankful, because getting something prematurely can be detrimental. This is no different than giving a ten-year-old the keys to your car. We all know nothing positive will come out of that scenario.

I remember a good friend's mother saying to me, "This business is never going to work until you get the inner you to reflect the outer ambitions and expectations that you desire."

Nothing about that statement made much sense to me at the time, but she was right. I had yet to learn that as human beings we live from the inside out, not from the outside in. This simply means the inner you—spirit, mind, heart and intentions—all must be carefully crafted and molded to produce the outer tangible results that we all are diligently searching for.

Unfortunately, we are only taught to spend our time, energy and effort on the external things; this is working the system of progress backwards. The mechanics of accomplishment tend to become more important than building your foundation, which is what the journey is all about.

Nothing ever worked FOR me until I started working ON me. My ambitions led me to do what most have tried before. I sought out all the self-help materials I could find and began to learn principles for success, how to build the right network and how to create wealth overall.

I had no problem portraying myself as the picture of success *externally,* but I wasn't really interested in becoming a better person *internally.* I wanted things to work for me without taking the time to transform myself into a person who was ready and able to receive those things. I tried to apply principles to an unstable foundation, and that just doesn't work. Occasionally, the principles alone will help you acquire something that may resemble success, but the façade pales in comparison to the real thing. I had studied all the principles and read all the books, but still felt like a hamster on the never-ending wheel to nowhere.

A principle (external) is only as good as the spirit/person (internal) that it comes into contact with. When a principle encounters someone who has not developed the proper environment that will allow it to grow, nothing really happens. This could be the reason why all the literature pushing the steps to success that fill our bookstores and flood the Internet doesn't work for everyone.

The principles represent the seed, and we are the ground. Now when the seeds are planted, they will only reach full healthy maturity if everything in and around that soil is conducive for it to fully produce. A lot of our seeds (principles) aren't growing properly because our internal ground (spirit, mind, heart, intentions) have not finished their cultivation process.

Life works as the result of a system of operation. If you violate that system in any way, then you will experience its negative effects. For example, if you have a vehicle that runs on gasoline, there is a system in place that governs how that vehicle operates. If you want that vehicle to produce (take you from point A to point B) then you have to give that engine gasoline in order for it to function. If you violate the system and put water in your gas tank, what happens? That vehicle will not produce the results you want. The system governing the vehicle doesn't care who you are, how you feel about it, or even if you agree with how it functions. If you want results, you must obey and work within the system.

Life operates in a similar way. Most of us have huge goals and dreams, along with great things we want to accomplish. The system of life must sculpt, mold and prepare us to receive and handle those desires. The journey often involves personal growth and sacrifice. It will involve stretching ourselves to the limit, frequently putting us in unfamiliar and uncomfortable positions. Those positions could work to change our perspective, help us to build a better attitude, show us how to deal with situations that would make others run for cover, and generally shape our thinking so as to produce solutions for any issues that will arise.

Everything we go through is a part of the process. The process will often involve this word: mind-set. Now I know all of us have heard this term before, but what does it really mean? Instead of saying *mind-set,* change it to *set your mind.* A play on that word truly helps to define it for what it implies and represents— what is your mind set on? Is it set only on creating wealth? Is it set on attaining power because most of your life you have felt powerless? Are your mind, heart and intentions truly set on the right things?

The process is designed to develop your belief system until it can't fathom anything but a purposeful, abundant life in every area. *When you don't embrace the process to mental, spiritual, and emotional elevation, your mind will never reach the level that will unlock what is inside those seeds and give them a chance to grow.*

So, the process involves taking the time to program your mind-set in order to create the belief system for the life you envision. In order to do that, you must control the way you think, which will control the way you choose. The decisions we make are the sum total of what our lives become. In order to program your mind to believe inwardly what you seek outwardly, you must pay attention to three E's.

Exposure is *the condition of being subject to some effect or influence.* What do you expose yourself to on a daily basis? Is television painting a perspective or telling you a vision of something that may not be conducive to what you want? Are you subjecting yourself to information that is the opposite of what you want to produce? If that is so, then you must immediately start only exposing yourself to information that corresponds with your desires, and not their opposite.

Environment is *the conditions that surround someone or something; the conditions and influences that affect your growth, health, progress and so on.* Consider this: Are your current conditions able to produce the results you desire? A tropical plant will never grow in a cold arctic climate, not because it doesn't want to, or because it doesn't have what it takes, but because the circumstances are not designed for it. Are you able to flourish in your current conditions and surroundings?

Experience is *the fact or state of having been affected by or gained knowledge through direct observation or participation.* What negative past experiences are dictating your future positive results? Are other people's experiences dictating or hindering your future outcome?

Life boils down to the art of consistently mastering yourself on every level. Over the years, I have discovered that to produce a truly successful and balanced life, attention must be given to: spirituality, physical health and wellness, professional purpose-driven achievement and building healthy relationships. Not addressing all of these areas will get you what I now refer to as one-sided success. What good is it to have all the money in the world but no genuine people to share it with? How fulfilled will you be if you build a great business or career, but it doesn't drive you or passionately wake you in the morning?

We have to start spending just as much time becoming better people personally as we do preparing the business plan and proposal letters. Then we create something far beyond wealth, fame, fortune or material things. We create a legacy and a level of significance that will leave the world forever changed long after we have transitioned on.

Failure is only a matter of perspective. Going back to that late Friday night when I was at a point in the process where quitting seemed like a viable option, I found myself in a church chapel. There was no sermon, no service, just a handful of people like me who needed something beyond ourselves: an answer, something to push us forward, or just a reason not to quit mid-journey.

As I sat in a pew all the way in the back of that dimly lit church, internally, something forever changed. You may not consider yourself the religious type and honestly neither do I; but I've always believed in a higher power. That night I prayed in such a way that I put a demand on that power to show me something. As I let my mind drift into meditation with tears rolling slowly out of my eyes, in that moment I heard: BORN II WIN. It gave me confirmation that I was destined for something great, and that this path I was on would also allow me to encourage other people to discover their greatness. BORN II WIN was the reassurance that no matter what I had gone through or what I was currently battling, the inevitable outcome would be victory. I don't believe the Creator is sending bad things our way to make us better, but when you are on this winning journey of life even something that appears to be meant for your demise will instead help you realize your true potential.

When you accept that you were BORN II WIN, born to conquer, born to overcome, then you know there is no such thing as failure. Your destiny to be great was set the day you took your very first breath. And from that first breath to the last, it is all designed for you to win. The things that happen throughout your process are just

174

preparation and training; never view this as failure. Who knows, those lessons may have been learned just so you'd be equipped to help someone else not quit while on their journey. No matter what you may be facing, know that it is temporary, meaning it is subject to change at any moment.

Defeat is a deception, and failure isn't real. Even though I believed I was at my breaking point that night, and it seemed like the end, it was really only the beginning of the greatness that would soon be revealed.

Since that night, BORN II WIN has turned into not just a statement but an inspirational speaking and empowerment company that business partner Monique Fluker and I were blessed to start. To date, BORN II WIN has shared this message of how the process is far from defeat on national and international platforms. All that I have faced so far on my journey was well worth it because it equipped me to live in my purpose.

I genuinely wish you well on your journey. And remember, no matter what happens along the way the end of your story is already written—you win. Why? You were BORN II WIN.

Winning is not just an option, it's simply a way of life.

R.J. Hodges is a professional speaker, certified life coach, certified practitioner in the healing art of Reiki and the creator of a coaching system known as L.I.F.E (Living in Full Existence) Education. He is the author of an audio book series, Winner Status *and the book,* You Can't Practice At The Game, The Art of Mastering You: Volume One. *R.J. is the founder and president of the inspirational speaking and empowerment company, BORN II WIN, specializing in personal and professional development with a focus on helping people master themselves in order to transition into their idea of success and fulfillment. Connect with R.J. at www.RJHodgesSpeaks.com, www. borniiwin.com and on youtube at www.youtube.com/user/borniiwin/ videos.*

CARMEN M. HERRERA

"HOW DID SHE GET HERE?"

I looked around the conference room and took stock for a moment. I nodded and smiled to myself as I thought, "I made it! Girl, you are exactly where you planned to be—in a room filled with success and money." Little did I know, it wasn't actually my plan, but He let me think it was, at least for now.

Despite the honor and the buzz of success in the room, I couldn't rid myself of that little bristle of annoyance at being eyeballed by all the men who couldn't accept that I was there. I had spent years busting my ass to propel myself to the top in a white male-dominated industry. None of their expressions read what they should have: *She must be damn good and amazing at what she does, because she's in the room with us.*

No matter how many times I showed up, it seemed to be a surprise. I could see it on their faces every time I made my confident, bold entrance. I could feel their irritation. Whether at a meeting in the local office or at national conventions from New York City to the hills of San Francisco, it was always the same. It was even worse when I received an award, especially an award based on high production for the year. It was so funny to see so many of them struggling to hold their composure. They just couldn't get it. Their expression was so obvious. "How did she get here?"

I would hold my giggles to myself thinking, "You go, girl!"

In addition to the disbelief, many times I found my carefully selected classy and professional business attire mentally peeled from my body. I was given that infuriating head-to-toe once-over with smirks and barely disguised, "come here" looks. They were all blind to how hard I had to work to get to where I was—I'm sure ten times harder than most of them—but they only saw the physical attributes. It wasn't just them; potential clients gave me the same treatment. I got so sick and tired of the sexual advances, not just mentally, but physically too.

I was determined to overcome this harassment and abuse because I understood that these were only distractions from a bigger plan.

Many men I worked with or tried to do business with could never get past the skirt. "This is all they can see?" I thought. "Somebody they want to sleep with, not somebody they want to work or do business with, or congratulate, like they would any man?"

Unfortunately, by this time, I was almost used to it. As a divisional vice president of a Fortune 500 global company, I was used to doing things for myself that other vice presidents wouldn't dream of doing—all because if I didn't I would be labeled as the

Many men I worked with or tried to do business with could never get past the skirt.

"pushy bitch." If one of my male counterparts asked our staff to do something for them, they would be met with, "Yes sir, right away sir." I could ask for the same thing, but it would be a problem. At times my own assistants would actually complain to the office manager that I was too pushy or demanding. I couldn't even get respect from the female staff who seemed as if they too could not believe I was right where I was meant to be—where I *deserved* to be. Many times the administrative support that I needed and paid for, I never got. But I was used to meeting opposition and coming back even stronger.

Our office had more than one hundred financial advisors while I was the only advisor of color, and for many years I was one of only three women. Though on the surface it appeared this disparity wasn't about racial prejudice, it was there. Don't get me wrong—the people I worked with were good people overall and a lot of them became good friends of mine. Unfortunately, they struggled with my invasion into their world.

Still, they seemed unable to comprehend how a young minority female could even be in the same room as them, let alone do their job as well as they did, and in some cases, better.

I come from a very strong, supportive family background. I was the only girl out of eight children; I always felt cherished because of that. Being the only girl actually helped me to succeed in a male-dominated industry. It motivated me to persevere and get these men to the realization that all of my brothers had eventually

I couldn't afford to feed us both.

reached: "She's a girl!" They had to eventually accept that, yes I was a woman and yes I must be *really* good. Please don't mistake my confidence as conceit, because it's not. It's just that I had to be better; I had to go the extra distance. I had to do more in order to stay in the game. That is why I'm confident in who I am and what I've accomplished.

That day in the conference room was one of many similar experiences I had over the course of my career in corporate America. Each time it happened I would tell myself, *I want to be in this business,* then hold my chin up just a little bit higher and let their looks roll off me as I continued to work harder and be the best I could. I kept telling myself, *I have to make it, I'm not a quitter—I am not going to fail. So I have to take it; I've endured far worse than a few suggestive looks and people not believing in me.*

My shift into the financial services industry came on the heels of corporate downsizing while I was working as an accountant for a law firm. I wanted to be a stockbroker ever since seeing the original movie *Wall Street* when I was young. I jumped into the opportunity headfirst, even though I had no clue it would be a hellish struggle to get to where I needed to be. The industry success rate is only twenty percent, and if you are a minority female that rate decreases by seventy-five percent, so you do the math. Unfortunately, I came to know that the hard way. Success wasn't going to just ring my doorbell, and a paycheck would not just appear in my mailbox on Fridays.

About a year after getting into the business, I was seriously struggling. If I was lucky I made nineteen thousand dollars, less than half of what I'd been making at the law firm. My daughter was very young, and there would be nights when I would make excuses for her to stay overnight with my parents or her dad so she

Knowing I'm walking in purpose is worth more than any paycheck.

had a warm place to sleep. Many times I had no gas or electricity; I would pile myself with blankets in front of my wood-burning fireplace at night, in order to not freeze to death in the brutal Wisconsin winters. There would be times when I was so low and out of frustration, I would say to God, "Really? Really, is this what you really have for me? Is this how you really want things to be?"

My first two years in the business I lost a lot of weight because the only food I was able to afford was bags of mixed frozen vegetables and hotdogs, *sometimes* chicken from Wal-Mart. I would ration the food to make sure my daughter had enough to eat because I couldn't afford to feed us both. I always sat at the dinner table with her and often she would ask in a soft, squeaky voice, "Mommy why you not eating?"

I would reply, "Baby, Mommy's not hungry; I ate already," which was a lie.

Though they didn't know quite how much I was struggling, people around me could see it. They'd tell me, "You're educated, you have degrees—you can go get a job anywhere."

There was a certain kind of pride behind my decisions—there really was no reason that I should have been nearly starving, I could have easily gotten another job. I would imagine hearing their reactions inside my head: *This is ridiculous! You can't even feed yourself! What are you doing? What's wrong with you?* Because I didn't want the negativity, I pretended that everything was okay, even though it wasn't. I had entered a brutal industry that was set up for me to fail if I believed in and followed the status quo. I was determined that I was not going to fail, so I pretended that everything was fine.

I was always motivated by the fact that I could make a difference, that I could help, that I could change things. I was fortunate to be doing something that my heart desired then and still desires now. I believe a lot of people work in industries and jobs by incident, accident or coincidence. Unfortunately, many people don't work or operate in their mission in life. That would *not* be my story.

Believing that I was walking the path of my calling was what motivated me above all else. When I helped someone, I would experience inner joy. It had nothing to do with money and everything to do with the smile or the relief on their faces, unknowingly expressing to me their gratitude for my help. I was determined to work in the financial industry helping people no matter what, and I never strayed from that. I knew that I wasn't supposed to give up, despite the sexual advances, the disrespect or the lack of—it was all just part of the process.

Despite being hungry and cold, when I helped a client, the inner joy and peace I felt assured me, "This is what you're supposed to be doing." I had to do whatever I had to do and go through whatever I had to go through, regardless of how bad things were. There are still times when things aren't the way I would choose them to be. Many times over the years I have been challenged with setbacks and obstacles trying to stop me from living in purpose. I continue to stay the course, not only to experience a better outcome for my family and me, but to also experience fulfillment of purpose. Knowing I'm walking in purpose is worth more than any paycheck. Some people would rather stay in a known bondage than pursue an unknown freedom, but not me.

So many times I just wanted to give up. With all the sexual advances, disrespect from my peers and staff, being hungry, cold and broke, it's a wonder I didn't. But that joy and sense of peace is what kept me in that conference room, despite the looks and the thoughts that I could practically hear: *Why would someone like you, a young minority female, want to do this? What could you possibly have to offer that we don't already have covered?* I knew then: What I had to offer was me!

Twenty-six years ago, I was a rare commodity in the financial industry. I realized early on that I was blazing a trail, and even through all the struggles, one of the things that comforted me

Desire, drive and determination
are key ingredients for winning.

then, and still does, is I wake up every morning, take myself out of the equation and remind myself, *This isn't about me—this is for those who will come after me; I am on an assignment.*

Someone had to take the persecution and get beaten up, and I was used to being knocked down and getting right back up again. I believed I was the one God trusted in to put there to change it all; I was the one who had been intentionally positioned for this particular mission.

Walking into your calling is not an easy task. As the Bible says, "To whom much is given, much is required." People can have careers and work in industries that they like, but not necessarily where their true purpose is, or where they bring the most value to a situation or to those around them. Though I'm in a good place, I'm good at my craft, I know my stuff and I'm confident in who I am and what I do, I still consider myself a work in progress. I've had the titles and the testimonials, and that is part of success, but really, I'm only halfway to leaving behind a meaningful legacy, a story that people will remember.

Going through the struggles of climbing the ladder of success taught me to be my best student. Every time I encountered a hill to climb or a valley to walk, it reinforced what I am supposed to be doing and gave me better understanding of the message I have to deliver. Those things had to happen to me so that I could pass on a message that would help others.

The financial service industry can be one of the toughest; any industry is tough when you start out—especially if, like me, you're a pioneer for your minority. It's never been about the money for me; I'm in it because my heart is in it. Every morning I get up and pray for who I can help, whose situation I can make better.

Know this: No matter what obstacles life brings your way, you can't give up or let them get in the way of your calling. Desire, drive and determination are key ingredients for winning. You can do what you want to do, go where you want to go and most important, be who God designed and desires you to be.

Picture yourself waking up tomorrow morning. What do you want to be waking up to? What is your goal at the end of your struggles, and even through climbing the hills and walking the valleys, won't it be worth it when you get there?

Carmen M. Herrera is the managing partner of CMHC Wealth Advisors LLC, an elite fee-based wealth consulting firm that offers specialized tax, retirement and estate planning strategies. Before starting her firm in 2010 she worked for AXA Advisors LLC, one of the world's largest financial service firms, as a financial consultant and divisional vice president.

Carmen is a dynamic keynote speaker and provides wealth education strategies through workshops and seminars. She is currently the board chair of National Sales Network (NSN) Houston chapter and is a member of several professional organizations. Start seeking the answers to your financial success by visiting www.CMHCWealth.com.

LARRY BOYER

THE BUSINESS OF YOU

Can you imagine walking into your boss's office and asking to be laid off? That's just what I was doing that summer day in 2008. Now, this was before the collapse of Lehman Brothers, before AIG and Fannie Mae and Freddie Mac needed bailouts—before all the bailouts. I'm an analyst and I had forecast that the country would lose two million jobs before the year was out. Despite that dire prediction, I wanted to be included in the coming round of layoffs.

As a principle economist at Freddie Mac, I had been hired to develop new cutting-edge risk models that were used for pricing all of the mortgages in the multi-family industry as well as for calculating the capital reserves the company needed to hedge against the risk. My team had developed the model, and now it was set in stone by government and corporate regulations. We weren't allowed to tweak it, even though we knew it needed improvement. My work had devolved into bureaucratic paper shuffling that others could do as just well.

As was the case for many people, I ended up feeling stuck. On one hand, my job was going no further and was no longer challenging me. On the other hand, it provided me with a steady paycheck that allowed me to support my family and live a comfortable but not extravagant life. And seeing the upcoming economic employment problems made it all the harder. *Should I continue drudging through the days, disengaged and risking poor performance reviews because I'm not mentally or emotionally engaged? Do I start looking for another job? If so, what kind of a job? I don't want to leave this one and end up in a worse situation.*

I had been raised in a solid working class family, taught to work and provide for my family. Enjoying the work was a secondary consideration. My father spent his entire thirty-five-year career as a lineman with AT&T, though in his last few years he was assigned a desk job he did not care for. At the time I didn't understand the subtle, yet powerful, influence his life experience had on shaping me and influencing me.

Fortunately, over the previous few years I had been investing in my own personal development, learning how to be more successful from some of the great business trainers, like Brian Tracy, and had enrolled in a coach training program with iPEC to help me

I ended up feeling stuck.

become a more effective leader. What I learned in the process over those several years, thousands of hours of training and more money than I'd care to admit, was how much my career was like a business.

As I learned more during the last two years, I started taking a hard look at my job from a new angle and saw that it no longer meshed with my values, my mission, my purpose in life.

The work I was doing had transformed from what was essentially the early stage development of a business to a more mature phase of business. My purpose is to bring people and ideas together to breathe life into new creation, especially through the use of analytics.

I came to understand how I built my personal success not just through my technical knowledge, but more importantly through my ability to help everyone around me become more successful, too. Armed with this knowledge, I began to develop a plan for a coaching business to help people with their careers in addition to my own analytics work.

Knowing what my career path needed to include to be successful, I had a new-found confidence. So, when I went to see my boss, I wasn't the least bit nervous. After all, what was the worst he could do: Fire me from a job that wasn't right and free me to do what I enjoy? He wasn't all that surprised, either. I had become increasingly disengaged from the work, and it had begun to show.

My boss had to consult with the human resources department and with the executives. It took a week before he told me I would not be laid off. "You can either re-engage with your work here, or leave," he said.

I was disappointed because it would now take longer to reach my goals than I expected, but the year I stayed was valuable. I have come to understand how there is a reason for every event, even if

There is a reason for every event.

it's not obvious in the moment. I spent the next year getting very specific about my next steps. During that time, I designed the business of me.

Through my career in developing and setting up business processes across functions I had become knowledgeable about a variety of business functions. As a team leader, I had become good at developing and expanding the talents and skills of my team members. I wanted to use that expertise as a career coach. While writing my business plan, I was struck again and again by the similarities between a business plan and a personal career plan.

A good business plan begins with a mission statement and a set of core values and so does a career plan. Businesses sell products and services; employees sell their services. Businesses generate revenue and pay expenses; employees get a salary and pay expenses. Businesses compete for sales; employees compete within the corporate environment for advancement or in the job market for employment.

Treating your own career as a business provides a structure and a discipline that people don't usually think about. Most people see career development as an afterthought. In most businesses, even when a career development process exists, it is given short shrift or even totally ignored. Employees might have to formally write out an individual development plan at the beginning of the year, but that's the last they see of it until the end of the year.

A business plan forces you to think about what you want to do, about your core values and purpose in life. It creates a sense of self-empowerment and self-responsibility. When you start to think about your career as your business, you realize that you're

When you treat your career as a business, you change your viewpoint.

responsible for it and that you get to choose. It's not that the company hires you, it's that you accept the opportunity to do this work for them and you can choose to move on at any time. Your thinking shifts and you move from the powerless to the powerful.

Once I realized that, two things happened. I began to notice the little triumphs in my work at Freddie Mac—things I failed to notice before—so that my job became more enjoyable. And having reconnected with my core values and purpose, I recognized the opportunity that best suited my mission when it appeared.

The use of a business plan connects both facets of my present work life. In my job as an economic and analytics consultant, I lead a team of twenty-five people, not only to pursue the analytical work, but also to develop the team internally and help them grow and progress. I apply these same principles working with clients in my career coaching business. And coming full circle, in my work, one of the things I do is help other people be more successful in their careers while solving their problems that require complex analysis.

Laura, one of my coaching clients, had been unemployed for thirteen months when I started working with her. This was right at the height of the Great Recession, and unemployment was at its highest levels. Within three months, we were able to change her viewpoint about looking for a job and on how to interview to be much more self-empowered.

As many people do, she thought getting a job was about being smarter and more experienced than everyone else. She believed she had to present a certain "professional front" that was not really who she was. By working together, we discovered more about what really energized her about accounting and were able to develop a strategy wherein she could feel good about presenting the real her. We asked, and answered, why would an accounting firm like her, rather than the image of a serious, straight-laced suit?

She identified what she wanted and was able to find a job that paid more than what she was expecting at a more prestigious firm than she thought would hire her. The key difference was that she understood for herself who she was and what was important to her, getting back to her values and mission and purpose.

And then she learned to communicate and portray that in her interviews, to be her genuine self. The businesses that liked that brought her in for interviews. They loved her personality because she was just being herself rather than pretending to be what she thought somebody in the accounting field should be. And because she was confident in who she was and projected that, the interviewers loved her.

Today, I am happier and more productive than ever. And because, like so many people, I spend most of my day at work, my job satisfaction also comes home with me.

I know the work I need to be doing to keep myself growing, motivated and fulfilled. I work in two businesses that complement each other and in both I help everyone I work with be more successful. I experience what is happening in the business world and the economy and translate that to how it impacts workers. I connect dots that few others connect and as a result I can help businesses and people prepare for the future, adapting as best they can to be successful. It is through my coaching work with

Success Rockets LLC that I get to help the most people, through my writings, online programs and individual coaching.

You have the power to define what it is that you want. You don't have to be the powerless person who's always applying for jobs, waiting for your work to be noticed, hoping you're chosen for the project you really want to tackle. When you treat your career as a business, you change your viewpoint so that you're looking for the right opportunity for you. It puts you in the driver's seat of your life and your career. You recognize that you're the one who gets to choose with whom you work, for whom you work and with whom you partner—not the other way around.

It's no longer the case that the companies are the powerful people, and you get to go begging for scraps. Turn it around; the companies are begging for scraps looking for people, and you're the one who gets to decide whether they're good enough for you.

The "business of you" is about applying the proven methodologies and discipline that successful businesses use to your life. Just as a business has executives, departments of finance, marketing, operations and more, so do you. A business sells products or services and so do you. You may have heard lots of people talk about being the CEO of your life or about the business of you, but who really tells you how to set up, structure and run the business of you?

Taking ownership of your career, your whole life even, and operating it like a business gives you power to control your destiny in ways that you can't really understand until you start to do it.

Larry Boyer is the premier career coach for early to mid-career professionals planning to advance into the project management, partnership, or executive levels. He has a fifteen-year history creating high-performing teams whose members have rewarding careers as executives, entrepreneurs, project managers and team leaders. Larry's unusual background crosses the spectrum of professional disciplines from the hard sciences to social sciences to human potential. Because of his interest and success in helping people create successful career paths, Larry is uniquely qualified to help select individuals and teams understand the new career dynamics of the twenty-first century and develop successful career strategies through his company, Success Rockets LLC.

Larry has a bachelor's degree in physics, a master's degree in economics and a master's degree in public administration with a concentration in environmental policy and management. He applied his unique combination of skills and experience to lead the development of innovative models that help government agencies and corporations achieve their financial and management objectives. Larry rapidly advanced through the ranks at Price Waterhouse and after five years moved on to Freddie Mac to the lead the development of a cutting-edge financial risk model that would bring together strengths across disciplines and structures. He then moved on to IHS where he took charge of the newly formed decision analytics team, expanding their project base and growing the staff for four years. He was then asked to lead a cross-functional effort to design a big data analytics platform that would meet the growing needs of his team and others across IHS.

Success Rockets offers coaching for individuals who are looking for proven methods to take charge of their careers and financial futures, as well as corporate training on leadership and staff development. Connect with Larry at www.SuccessRockets.com.

ANTOINE D. MOSS, PHD

BE THE CEO OF YOUR DREAMS

I t sounds cliché, but it's true: life is what you make of it. When you look at my upbringing on paper—had a teenage, single mother; attended under-served schools; lived in urban poverty surrounded by drugs, crime and gang activity—it could have turned out pretty bad for me. I saw young men and women in my neighborhood fall to drugs and crime, drop out of school and get caught up in the legal system, their lives seemingly pre-determined from an early start.

But when you look at the life that I've created for myself by sheer will, it's pretty impressive, especially in comparison. I was the first person in my family to graduate from college with a bachelor's degree. I went on to earn a master's degree and a PhD, with leadership being my focus of research and study. Currently, I'm a program manager at NASA, where I help create and manage federal executive policies that will improve the environment and living conditions for our country. Being a young leader at NASA is not too bad for a kid from the wrong side of town.

While I know that what I've been able to accomplish is extraordinary, I also know that it's possible for anyone else to accomplish. Anyone can come from a tough background and achieve their dreams; you just have to want it. I like to call it "becoming the CEO of your Dreams."

I like to define CEO in the context of you being the Creator of Excellent Opportunities. Despite what you may have experienced in your life, *you* are responsible for creating positive opportunities in your life. They're certainly not just being handed out regularly; you have looking them and, when that fails, make them happen.

My wonderful mother, Jeanette, was a teen mom at the age of sixteen; she then had two more children, each two years apart. My brothers and I didn't grow up with a father in the home to set the example for how a man in a household should behave. Instead, we had a loving mother who, despite all of the disadvantages she faced, including dropping out of high school and a stint in a highly toxic and abusive relationship, one that robbed her of her self-esteem and self-worth, was still working herself as hard as she could to do right by us.

My two brothers and I all shared one room; we shared until I was fifteen years old, in fact. It wasn't unusual for us to pick up and move to a new place every two years or less. Once, we were homeless and had to live in a shelter for a time, but we were always

You are responsible for creating positive opportunities in your life.

together, and we always had my courageous mother setting the example for us of never giving up. She wanted us to do better than she had. She wanted us to excel in school, maybe go on to college, anything that was better than the limited experience she was able to provide for us.

What my mother maybe doesn't realize is that by her courage, by her never giving up and always trying to do right by her sons, she set an example for me.

She made me think, "I want to do better than this," and I wanted to do that for her. She encouraged me to match her hard work and ultimately to live the type of life that would make her proud.

To be the CEO of your dreams, you must intentionally create a positive environment that will lead to positive outcomes.

With my mom working as much as she did, many of the responsibilities of the house were up to me. I was the one who made the most frequent trips to get groceries with our food stamps, I would be the one who would skip school to be home for any repairs or deliverymen to enable my mother to keep working, and I would be the one she could lean on when my brothers needed help. I had to rise to the task of being a leader early in my life, but this was one of the best lessons for me.

In elementary school, a group of us boys in the neighborhood banded together, and many of our peers referred to us as a street-level gang. We thought of ourselves as a posse or clique, since we weren't what most people associate with the term "gang," although we did have "gang-like" T-shirts and hats with our group's name

**If you seek help, there truly are
people who are willing to offer it.**

on it. We were good kids, well liked by our peers, into sports and our schoolwork, and we stuck to each other like glue. By middle school, we settled on what to call ourselves, a nickname that folks in my old neighborhood still use to refer to us: 6 Deep. Guess how many of us there were? Well, we originally started off with about six guys, but by high school, well over fifteen guys were associated with 6 Deep.

What this group of young men provided for me is immeasurable. There is no mistaking the value of a child growing up with a caring mother, but as a young man, I understood early on that I didn't have a steady male in my life to model the right sort of behavior to help me as I grew up. In this group of friends, we were able to provide some of that for one another. We had each other's backs day to day, looked out for younger kids and pushed one another to always try to top our latest achievement.

We couldn't be everything to each other, but I was fortunate to have a few male relatives, mentors, teachers and coaches, as well as some of the older young men in our community who could fill in those gaps, and who were men I could look up to and aspire to be like.

My uncle and grandfather were there for me, and by the time I was in the eleventh grade I was able to reconnect with my father. Both my football and basketball coaches let me hang around them, ask them questions and observe how they handled their lives, how they met their challenges in life with grace and acumen.

This taught me that if you seek help, there truly are people who are willing to offer it. When I was younger, I asked a lot of questions. Some would call that curious, but my mother called that plain being nosy. Nosy or not, I had an itch to learn everything I could and was fortunate enough to have gentlemen in my life who took me under their wing to make sure that I did. I was so persistent, in fact, that it became known by some of the older folks in my community that I was the kid for any camps or seminars they'd

**Have an ever-present desire to
learn and improve yourself.**

heard about. They'd make sure I knew about the opportunity with the hope that I could attend and satiate my growing desire to learn and develop as a man.

Coaches would make sure I knew about conferences coming up, conferences with motivational speakers or a message that would continue to fuel my fire to do better, to keep climbing, to realize my dreams. Teachers who knew about my good leadership skills and how curious I was would think of me when it came time for development opportunities, like a summer camp or classes that focused on leadership, education or self-motivation. Success is simple. The more you learn, the farther you will go.

At the time, I was trying to understand who my identity was as a man, and those thoughtful older people who mentored me set an example for me to follow, which helped me become a leader in my own right.

With a good group of relatives and friends, coaches and mentors looking out for me, and a hard-working mother, I made every moment count. I graduated high school, and was honored by my graduating class with the "Most Likely to Succeed" superlative. Several of my 6 Deep friends went on with me, and a few others entered the military. We'd done it: We had each other's backs; we kept each other moving forward toward the goal of doing better than just plain living. I know without a doubt that if we hadn't had each other's backs, if I hadn't made the point of making those around me aware of my desire to move forward in life, then I and my fellow 6 Deep friends would have been "lost in the sauce," as we'd say. The leader of 6 Deep, Ronald, would regularly remind us that true relationships in life last forever—and this slogan has been our mantra till this day.

The foundation that I intentionally created helped me excel in college, going on to get graduate degrees until I ended up where I am today, working at NASA with some of the greatest minds in the world, all of us working together to make the world a better place. Leadership opportunities had always been something I'd looked for, and it paid off with me joining the Center Operations Department, becoming project manager of development transportation policies at NASA Glenn Research Center. One of my mentors, who is an astronaut, revealed some of his success secrets to me and these tips enabled me to accelerate my career at NASA.

Getting to this point in my life, coming from where I did, is a dream come true. I had been my own CEO of my dreams all along without realizing it.

I've been able to discern what steps I and my fellow 6 Deep crew were able to follow to achieve better lives, how we managed to transform our minds for success.

Step One: Become a leader. Leaders should be the light to knowledge and exposure, as opposed to the door to failure and closure. Growing up in my underserved community, I encountered many bad leaders. A good leader empowers other people to bring out the best in themselves. Like with my group of friends, we were able to influence each other, helping each of us continue to improve, keeping each other on the right track.

Step Two: Have confidence. You can't be afraid to ask questions, to reach out to others seeking opportunities. Believe in yourself despite where you came from. I came up out of poverty to work for an agency that has brought forth some of the greatest achievements in human history. If I can do it, of course you can, too!

Step Three: Invest in yourself. On a daily basis, you should make learning and bettering yourself a priority. Your mind and spirit are worth every moment you can dedicate to your own betterment. The great Neil deGrasse Tyson has said, "I live by two philosophies: Know more today about the world than I knew yesterday, and lessen the suffering of others." If you're acting as a leader in your community, if you're bettering yourself and encouraging those around you to be their best, you'll be well on your way to achieving your dreams.

Step Four: Don't rest on your laurels. Be in competition with yourself. You reached one of your goals? Terrific! Now, how can you get to that next level? Contribute at your highest peak in order to get closer to your dreams. Be a living testament to show other people they can do this.

My lovely mother who worked as a housekeeper all my life— she's still at it, too!—had a simple dream that she once thought was unobtainable: to own her own home. Well, I'm happy to say that my mother was able to buy her own home after years of working and saving. It may be a simple dream, but it was a good one and it was hers. Since my mother was unable to complete high school because she was the teenage mom to three boys, I gave her my bachelor's degree when I graduated from college.

Now is the time to create excellent opportunities for yourself and be your own CEO of your dreams. Say with me: "I'm the CEO of my dreams and there's nothing you can do about it."

Antoine D. Moss, PhD, is the first member of his family to graduate from college with a bachelor's degree and is the youngest African-American to have graduated from Cleveland State University's College of Urban Studies & Public Affairs' doctorate program. He is a nationally recognized motivational speaker, is the author of a book titled Learn to Intern CEO Style: 71 Leadership Principles That Got Me and Now YOU Money, A Free Graduate Degree, and Respect! *and acts as a career coach. Antoine works at NASA as a program manager, working on developing policies that will improve our environment. He's also contributed to over thirty articles for* Black Enterprise *magazine and is the founder and CEO of CEO Style Consulting, LLC., whose mission is to empower organizations and professionals to reach their full potential. Connect with Antoine at www.AntoineMoss.com.*

KELVIN L. McHENRY

THE 50-50 RULE

If you look at me, you'll see an average guy. I've faced a lot of setbacks, from divorce to injury to being passed over for a promotion. And I have every secret in the book—I've read the books, asked the questions, tried to figure out why the rich are rich and the poor are poor and what the big secret to success is. Better yet, the secret to achieving the American Dream.

I've noticed that all of the so-called "secrets" only create a situation where you accept that there are haves and have-nots. And we all know it; we all have family members and friends in our own situation. We know some people beyond that who are better or worse off. That's how things are, traditionally. I have discovered how to surpass that in a practical way.

I was just over seventeen years old when I joined the Army National Guard. I was a kid from the poor side of town, and the bonus they offered sounded good. So I shipped off to boot camp and began my training on things I had never experienced, from weapons to navigation to articles of war. And as I rose through the ranks, I began teaching the thing I'd only just learned myself.

At one time, we had a resident "smart guy." He knew everything. But he transferred out, and I had to take over his class on radio troubleshooting, which I was not familiar with. So I began to research, in particular with my friend Sergeant Jones, who taught that subject like a pro. I figured I could get the goods from him and do better when I had to teach my guys.

But Sergeant Jones wouldn't share his lesson plan with anyone. He believed that because he had to go through the trial and error process to get there, then everyone else had to sweat their own blood and tears to get there, too. So I had to put up with the guys giving me a hard time as I unnecessarily fumbled through and made mistakes that others before me had already made. I told myself then that I would never sit idly by watching others struggle to perform a task that others had previously performed.

I began to pay attention to the way things were done and I noticed a pattern. It was a pattern of dependency—one person would be identified to perform a task to standard, and then that person would keep it a secret until forced to let it go. Then someone else would come in, and they'd have to go through the learning process all over again, making mistakes while they learned what the person before them could have easily told them all along.

This brings us to the 50-50 Rule.

The 50-50 Rule is a practical science similar to Newton's laws: what goes up must come down, for every action there is an equal and opposite reaction. The 50-50 Rule simply states that given a task any fifty people, regardless of background, can all perform

I would never sit idly by watching others struggle.

the same task. Some will accomplish it faster, some will get there slower and some will require more or less help to there, but in the end they will all achieve the same standard. Given this fact, if know everyone can reach the same standard, that is fifty percent, why do we start from zero? Why not start from fifty percent and work forward from there?

The 50-50 Rule starts with percentages. When we know nothing about a topic, we're at zero percent. While we learn that topic, perfect our skills and, most importantly, discover what's already known about that topic, we go from zero to fifty. Once we've learned what others before us have learned, we start over at fifty percent—by then we've reinvented the wheel. For instance, I learned on my own what my friend Sergeant Jones already knew about radio troubleshooting, what he could have told me. That's my first fifty percent.

The second fifty percent—from fifty to one hundred—is what I could build on that myself. The first fifty percent is our foundation; it's our benchmark or standard. It begins with what we bring to the table, and we all bring something. The percentage you bring is usually found in your own strengths and life experiences. Therefore, evaluate yourself first, determine what percent you have.

**We put more priority on hard
work than on smart work.**

It could be ten percent, twenty percent or even thirty percent if the Lord has so blessed you. From here the journey begins, searching for what you need to get to fifty percent. If you only lack ten or twenty percent you might be able to achieve fifty percent rather quickly. Regardless, the point is not that the information may be given to you or shared with you, but the fact that you were seeking it, which in itself makes you deserving of it. I relate this to the bible verse that states: Ask and it shall be given unto you); seek, and you shall find; knock and the door shall be opened (Matthew 7:7 and Luke 11:9).

The other part is the obligation: To whom much is given, much is required (Luke 12:48). Therefore, I conclude leaders have an obligation to give back and share what they have learned. I always say that a leader who doesn't produce other leaders may need to reconsider whether he or she is a leader at all. Sharing life knowledge raises the bar across the board forcing everyone to work from a higher standard.

The second fifty percent is where we find our dreams, our goals, our natural talents and our purpose in life. Most people spend a lifetime of trial and error to achieve their first fifty percent, yet never reach it. Some may try to bypass the first fifty percent, eager to receive the benefits of the second fifty percent, only to run into a road block or get stuck in a position unable to climb out. Some find themselves running from here to there in search for the way ahead.

The truth shared in my 50-50 Rule provides you the breakthrough you need: the way ahead and the knowledge to overcome what were insurmountable hurdles. My 50-50 Rule is the resource you need to fill the gap; once you have it you will overcome those obstacles. You will soar like eagles.

My research has revealed that the second fifty percent comes a lot easier than the first. The second fifty percent is where your life purpose is, where your natural talents flourish; it's a place where your creativity can be applied. The bottom line is: The second fifty percent comes more naturally to you. The second fifty percent is more an internal approach, while the first fifty percent relies more on external factors.

No matter what, your natural talent will allow you to operate more comfortably in this zone. Although you will continue to rely on the first fifty percent, because once you know it works, you never want to find yourself operating below fifty percent.

My 50-50 rule applies to almost any situation in life.

You don't have to make the same mistakes everyone else before you already made. You just learn from them and get to your fifty percent as fast as possible, so you can start expanding on what is already known. The military is great at this. However, they seem to focus it on large scale, collective operations more than individual efforts. My 50-50 Rule is applied at the individual level.

When I was a senior enlisted advisor, I was fielding many complaints and grievances regarding soldier promotions. When I researched, I discovered several areas of conflict. Some employees expected administrators to submit them for a promotion; others were required to submit to the administrators themselves, only to find out they hadn't submitted the data on time. It was a mess—no one knew the proper way to go about getting their promotion, because everyone had a different way of doing it, and the secrets were so seldom shared.

So, I applied the 50-50 Rule—I put together all the promotion standards which had previously worked and consolidated that information into a spreadsheet. I called it an NCO (non-commissioned officer) Calendar. It contained policies, manuals, worksheets and deadlines; it told what you needed to submit and when. It took the guesswork out of it for everyone, soldiers

**You can start expanding on
what is already known.**

and administrators alike. Once that was done, dialogue was generated between all parties, and the secrets started to be shared. Grievances went down, and now soldiers knew exactly what it takes to get a promotion. It was simply a matter of sharing what had already been developed. With the distraction removed it allowed soldiers to focus on their missions instead of administrative matters.

The 50-50 Rule puts everyone on an even keel—people from all walks of life, whatever their background. If they all start with the same information, they can all achieve the same results, accomplish the same task. It might be slower for some, some might need more help than others, but everyone will be able to reach the same standard for whatever operation is needed. This way, everyone "has it;" the bar is raised and you only have one standard. There are no more have-nots—everyone has the opportunity to succeed.

This is how I became an aircraft mechanic. I started out in manufacturing, but I moved to working for an aircraft carrier. I knew nothing about that, and my formal training required that I obtain an airframe and power plant license from a school of aviation maintenance and technology. This was considered a license to learn. Aircraft was very high tech and constantly being ungraded with new high tech circuitry and components.

Naturally, I had to learn about these things—and there is only so much you can learn from books. I did that part, and the rest I had to learn from people who had already done it. So I voluntarily cross-trained in three skills: mechanical structures, systems and avionics.

Most of my success in transitioning into each one of these skills came from volunteering to help people working in that skill set. That allowed me to observe, up close and personal, the tricks of the trade and get tips from the masters. Add this to your book of learned skills: In addition to the theories of operation, I had my full fifty percent. From then on, I could work from fifty to one-hundred percent, adding on to what everyone already knew—including me.

I believe we are unnecessarily hindering our own progress. We say that because someone else had to sweat the blood and tears to get there, then everyone must do the same. But that's close to the old saying that insanity is repeatedly doing the same thing and expecting different results. We force people to make mistakes by doing the same things over and over again instead of just giving them the resources to skip over that part.

We put more priority on hard work than on smart work. We can all be the "smart guys and girls." We just need to seek the information we need to receive it.

How do you get the first fifty percent? By asking for it. Everyone can get to at least fifty percent by seeking out the knowledge of a topic that others have. It goes beyond theory in books—real experience is needed, whether that's second hand or not. Someone has to experience it first—that experience can be passed along, it doesn't have to be replicated.

So whatever your goals, if you connect somehow with those who have achieved your goals already, you can learn the secrets. Then you get to the part where you really succeed, where you achieve goals and reach higher levels than you ever thought you could. This is the fifty to one-hundred range, where you tread new ground and blaze your own trail. This is where you find what no one before you has found.

Great people, great leaders and great organizations operate from fifty-one to one hundred percent. With my 50-50 Rule, you can become a great leader, too

That's how I got to be highest enlisted rank in the United States Army. As a senior NCO. I oversaw the health and welfare, education, morale and discipline of all NCOs. I planned and coordinated resources and management of training programs that prepared, developed and improved the readiness of seven hundred and twenty personnel. And this reached farther, to their families. I oversaw all of it.

In seeking this position, I had to invest many hours observing, taking notes and listening to the pros and cons of how my predecessors had carried out their duties. The things that were successful, I captured and documented as such. The things that turned out horribly, I captured and documented how I wanted to do them differently, more successfully. And this all took place before I could even think of becoming the senior NCO. I had to gather the information before my promotion went through so that I could do my job to the best of my ability—so that I could operate in the fifty to one-hundred zone and find my purpose.

And I did it. You name it—NCO education, health and welfare, physical fitness, leadership, communication, evaluation reports, promotions, accountability, I became responsible for it. And it was never explained to me the way I've explained it to you. But it was instrumental in my preparation to achieving the highest enlisted rank. And it's been a great teaching tool I have used to share and help prepare my subordinate leaders on their journeys up as well.

Rewards and recognition came all along the way and I have many. Some from my military service, community service and civilian work. These recognitions are affirmation you're on the right track.

You can achieve your goal. Making it to that fifty percent takes work, but less work than the trial and error method. Everyone can do it, because it's already been done before. And once reached, then you can hit your prime level of operation. You have to observe, gather critical information, identify patterns, capture those patterns, document and critique them, apply them, revise them and then you can finalize your documentation and hit your fifty percent and beyond. From then on, you'll be one of "the greats" operating in the fifty to one hundred percent range.

It is here you will find your purpose.

Kelvin McHenry is a retired Command Sergeant Major, with more than thirty-two years of service in the Army National Guard and eight years of active duty service. He is a combat veteran, currently serving as an aviation maintenance supervisor for a major airline, and has demonstrated a life of service holding volunteer positions in several community organizations. He is the author of The 50-50 Rule to Successful Leadership. *Connect with Kelvin at www.Vizspace.com/ ProGreenServices.*

JANICE E. BISHOP CARTER

THE AWESOME POWER OF CONFLICT

My son, a successful high school graduate and gainfully employed in local government, ended up divorced and homeless. My daughter, also a successful high school graduate, became an unwed mother at age twenty. *Oh, my gosh! Both my children have become statistics,* I realized.

It would have been easy to blame their problems on their absentee fathers. Both of my ex-husbands were successful men—one was an educator, the other an FBI agent. I kept them informed about their children's progress in life.

There were occasional birthday cards, but no consistency. Neither of them attended or acknowledged baptisms or high school and college graduations. My children tell me now that they felt hurt, but having a loving family helped them not feel so abandoned.

I remembered the saying, "All you have is what you have and what you have is all you need." I would not let my children down. I would step up my leadership as a parent. I knew that real leadership doesn't order or demand, real leadership inspires. My own education had been deferred, helping one husband and then another through college and then raising children while working and being active in the community.

Now it was time to lead by example, to inspire my children. I returned to school. And that changed my life in ways I could not have predicted.

While earning my bachelor's degree in business management, I learned about the Strengths, Weaknesses, Opportunities, Threats (SWOT) model that businesses use to plan for sustainability and

I would step up my leadership as a parent.

success and to work through conflicts and crises. *A family is an organization, too. And a family also needs sustainability for success and a method for conflict resolution*, I reasoned. So, using the SWOT model as an inspiration, I developed the Phantom Family Model.

The Phantom Family Model applies to any family; in my family we used it this way:

- **Strengths** – We looked at the successes of the absent dads, not at their failure to parent.
- **Weaknesses** – We saw their weaknesses as an opportunity to develop empathy and to learn forgiveness.
- **Opportunities** – We focused on developing skills to manage interpersonal conflicts, creating win-win opportunities by using collaboration, compromise, avoidance and less competition.
- **Threats** – We analyzed the threats to our peace to know when to avoid compromise and when to collaborate, negotiate, mediate or use less competition through life's struggles and conflicts.

Like any good writer, the Author of Life thrusts us into conflict, struggles, crises to see what we're made of, to give us the opportunity to transform and evolve and become all we're meant to be. Conflict is inevitable; you're always going to receive it, be in the midst of it. The way to drive it and win is to put it in a system, a model. Most people perceive conflict as a hit that knocks you down. A model like the Phantom Family Model let me catch the fiery darts and transform them in my hand and then use that energy as fuel for transformation.

You can apply the SWOT model to any conflict. In whatever arena—family life, business, social groups—conflict is never an absolute good or bad thing; it's an inevitable situation that shall happen. It has the potential for learning and innovative solutions. The key is to understand your character and temperament and the character types of those with whom you interact. If the relationship has value, it's time to bring the conflict to the negotiation table.

To SWOT out relational conflict, you must first know your own strengths, weaknesses, opportunities and threats. Then you can

**Like any good writer, the Author
of Life thrusts us into conflict.**

transform relational suffering and pain for family, business or any personal relationships.

First you must realize that the other person in the conflicted relationship does not have those same strengths, weaknesses, opportunities or threats. We're alike in many ways but also equally different.

Differences make the world exciting and should be embraced. If everyone looked alike and thought the same, without the variables of our personalities and traits, it would be very boring.

I had two failed marriages. However, we shared collaborative success in that I helped plan, organize and direct my husbands' missions to obtain their college degrees. Twice, I deferred my college vision to support them. This style of resolution is called "accommodating;" when used too often, it creates conflict and resentment. I was left questioning: *When would I ever get my turn? And what would I be if I had someone to support my personal interests in the way I supported my husbands' goals?*

I thought I had satisfying relationships because I was fulfilling my own sense of duty to others. But I never negotiated about my personal needs or advocated for myself. And I wondered why my relationships fell apart. I was not happy; I was suffering disappointment and pain. I did not tell my partners what I wanted or needed. Like many others I've consulted with, I expected that, if they loved me, they should know what I needed.

When you know your strengths and weaknesses, your opportunities and strengths, you can ask for the support and help you need. You can expect your partners, family, friends and associates to encourage you in your endeavors.

Each of us has our own personal truth, formulated through life experiences that contribute to our beliefs and value systems. It doesn't make anyone right or wrong; it just makes it what it is. However, this is the lens each of us uses to filter everything in the world through our assumptions and expectations. The problem with this is, it supports a model for creating conflict.

**We change behaviors through
conflict resolution.**

Unclear definitions of responsibility, limited resources and conflicts of interest are major sources of conflict. Conflict will arise over decisions made or actions taken in disputed territory. Competition for time, money, space and so on will lead to interpersonal, unit or interdepartmental conflict. When an individual is more concerned with their personal goals and loses sight of their inter-dependent responsibilities, conflict will arise. Conflict is often caused by differences in preferred methods, priorities and personal styles.

When you have misunderstandings with people who think, prioritize and communicate differently, do your SWOT analysis to accept and know your strengths, weaknesses, opportunities and threats within your relationship with this particular individual. Allow them to be who they are and accept that you have the right to be who you are.

The three most important things I have learned are: We all have our own truth; we see through different lenses; and our varied personalities are what they are and influence our behavior. People don't have to change, but behaviors can be changed so that we can all have peaceful and satisfying experiences in every area of our lives.

We change behaviors through conflict resolution. Conflict is painful, but it also tenderizes you and gives you compassion to look at both sides. You need to get knocked down sometimes. It hurts, but sometimes you just have to go through it. When we are in a conflict or struggle, in hard times, we remember or we decide what direction we're going to take. We show our mettle by just sticking to it and getting through it. And when all the parties in a conflict understand their strengths, weaknesses, opportunities and threats, conflict resolution can be a powerful engine for healing and growth.

Janice E. Bishop Carter earned her bachelor's degree in business management and her master's in conflict management from Sullivan University in Louisville, Kentucky. She worked in law enforcement for twenty-nine years and supervised the Jefferson County Telecommunications system for police, fire and medical emergency response. Janice founded ARM Communication Group, LLC, which empowers clients in advocacy, research and marketing to exploit opportunities to improve the quality of their community or personal lives. She is an inspirational speaker and is currently planning her first book. She was the second elected, three-term female president in her community for the oldest national civil rights organization, Louisville Branch NAACP. Connect with Janice at www.JaniceBishopCarter.com.

ELAINE GINN

HEAR YOUR HEART, MIND YOUR MIND, LOVE YOUR LIFE

How would you describe your day today? Was it good or bad? Was it fantastic or terrible? Were you successful or did you fail?

I do not take my moments for granted. Each day I wake up is a blessing to be cherished. You would think that would have been my attitude all of my life. I have always been a positive-minded individual, mostly focusing on the half of the glass that was full.

I do remember, however, an interview with a man on a news magazine show such as *60 Minutes* in the 1970s. The subject was a positive-minded businessman. He was so positive that, when asked to describe his worst day, he declared he had never had a bad day in his life. That so struck me, that this man couldn't even recognize a bad day when he had one.

It just seemed abnormal. Everybody has good days and bad days. He seemed out of touch with reality. But, when pressed by the interviewer to describe just a part of one day that was a teeny bit bad, he maintained his original assertion. That puzzled me for many years. I wrote the guy off as delusional. Now, I have come to adopt his philosophy.

What I did not realize when I was younger is that nothing is inherently good or bad until I assign a meaning to it. That was a huge paradigm shift for me, because I had been raised in an environment where concepts, events, conditions and behaviors had meanings of their own, accepted at their predetermined value without need for further investigation. It was a black-and-white world, which made it easy to navigate, but not necessarily compassionate or in alignment with principles of human engagement that could lead to better understanding.

I discovered that there were many possible interpretations for any given situation. If someone insults me, I could be hurt or offended if I choose, or I could choose to view the comment as an independent opinion that did not necessarily have anything to do with me, but was rather the other person's idea regarding something they perceived about me, an idea that might or might not be of any value to me in making decisions about my life. It was my decision whether to be depressed for days or to dismiss the comment as irrelevant. That was a crucial paradigm shift for me.

Therefore, if I have a day that includes missed appointments, low productivity, a minor traffic accident, a delay in getting a crucial document, interruptions and no breakfast or lunch, I could be tempted to call that a "bad" day. Or, I could choose to focus on the assignment I completed, the unexpected letter from an old friend, the long-negotiated contract that a new client signed, the police person who handled the accident with such kindness and

**Each day I wake up is a
blessing to be cherished.**

the fact that the sun was shining. Our days are filled with a wide variety of encounters. We get to choose what we want to emphasize. I can now understand why the man never had a bad day, although someone else might have looked at any number of the days of his life and labeled them as bad.

Now I can look at days I might have been tempted to label as bad at the time through the old "retrospecto-scope" and see that great good came out of those days, too. My excruciating divorce led to meeting my children's father, and I wouldn't have wanted to miss that vast storehouse of joy and rich experiences and the delightful grandchildren who ultimately resulted from what seemed to be an unbearable unfolding of events.

Not only is there always something good in everything, if we but allow ourselves to see it, we can avoid the emotions of anger, resentment, pain, guilt and stress, which manifest in our physical bodies, leading to disease, increased difficulty in relationships and decreased life expectancy. Whew! That alone is reason enough to make the effort to find the good.

The support my parents gave me early on shored me up for what was looming ahead. My first husband, a doctor, had career plans for me to be a hospital nurse. When I accepted a position as an administrative assistant in a school of nursing, he decided I no

I got very sick very fast toward the end.

longer fit his image of a proper wife. John was adamant, "When we got married, I thought you would be a nurse, working on the ward in a hospital, and we would be able to talk with each other about our experiences."

"But, John," I countered, "I don't plan to forget everything I know, just because I will be working with students instead of patients. We can still talk about medicine."

He had convinced himself I was no longer the woman he had loved. It was truly a life-changing day when he moved into his own apartment a month before our third anniversary. I was absolutely devastated.

Now, it seems like such a petty disagreement. But that was the end of our marriage. I had never met anyone who was divorced. That just didn't happen in my family. My whole world changed. Here I was, a divorced woman at twenty-five. Embarrassed and alone, I was clueless about what was coming next. I had thought I had it all figured out. I was a doctor's wife, secure and happy. *Now what?* Everything was up for grabs. I was so ashamed. In 1973, it was far more of a stigma than it is today.

217

I survived, however, and I moved on. Not only did I remarry successfully, I moved one thousand miles away, found a totally new career teaching at a university, had two children and accomplished many of my hopes and dreams, including writing my first book. Then, the world collapsed around me: another divorce and a life-threatening illness requiring a liver transplant. After twenty years of marriage this time, I was such a wreck. My vision of our grown children bringing the grandchildren to visit on holidays and my husband and I growing old together and traveling was shattered. We were divorced a year before I got the transplant. It was time to start over again.

And, I did, leaving the university and moving two thousand miles this time to another career and a new life. Six years into this experience, my parents, then in their early eighties, were beginning

I truly see I never had a bad day.

to have aging and health problems, so I moved back two thousand miles to be there for them. Eventually, I moved into their home to provide full-time assistance with myriad needs. I would do that again in a heartbeat, because it was a one-time opportunity to show them exactly how much they meant to me. Mom died first, and Dad followed a little over a year later.

Most recently, I moved again, this time to be near the Mayo Clinic in Florida, for yet another transplant. This time, I needed another liver and a kidney to boot! More challenges came up, as I dealt with hallucinations, paranoia and many other issues I did not face with the first transplant. For the first time, I realized it was possible I might not make it.

Day after unending day, there were new unpleasant diagnostic and treatment-related assaults on my frail little body. I got very sick very fast toward the end. I truly did not want a life as miserable as mine was at that point, so while I did not really want to die, I was at peace with that as a possible outcome. I thought, *I'm certainly no good to myself or anyone else in this condition.*

As the days wore on, I always hoped for the best, but was beginning to despair. I was exhausted and wondered how long I could hang on. Through all of this, I wound up with some great stories to tell, a renewed sense of urgency and a profound appreciation for each breath I draw. I also have far more compassion for others who are experiencing similar difficulties. And, with the help of my daughter Brea, my brother Terry and the rest of my family, I have been triumphant. The whole saga of caring for my parents and my transplant experience is told in my latest book, *Patchwork*.

I mention these challenges through the years only so you can appreciate the fact that I did not lead a charmed life. I even left out a third divorce. I was married a total of thirty-three years and don't regret a minute of those experiences, because each thing that happened in my life has added to my understanding, coping skills and appreciation for each day.

Looking back, I truly see I never had a bad day. I have had sad days, painful days, growth-producing days that weren't really enjoyable. Every one of those days was a good day. Now, I can see that each day that I once thought was bad was an important step leading me to where I am. Each of my ex-husbands helped me to understand that there was so much that I needed to learn, including knowing myself better. Each aspect of my illness provided insights and developed my compassion for others. Each disappointment showed me what didn't work well, so I can hone my skills to include only those that do lead to success. All of my difficult experiences have taught me humility and the strength of "thriver-ship."

My kidney and liver transplant surgery was four years ago. Each "bonus" year, each of my bonus minutes, is so precious to me. I have an unstoppable mission to make this gift valuable not only to myself, but to others as well. I wake up with a sense of urgency, not a frenzied, frantic urgency, but a deep-in-my-soul passion to share what I can with this amazing world. I want other people to know this sense of peace and purpose for themselves, for each person has a unique quality that benefits others and the world at large.

Anything I do puts out a vibration to the world, and I want it to be a resonant harmony that uplifts and supports individuals and the sense of peace and good will in the world.

Having a liver and kidney that work make me so acutely aware of my blessings. This heightened awareness is largely due to this new perspective I have. When I think about it, there were many years of my life when all of my organs were functioning perfectly, yet I did not feel this sense of urgency and expansive appreciation of all there is to enjoy. They say, "You don't know what you've got 'til it's gone." I implore you not to wait: Savor each flavor; bless each relationship; attend to your tasks with vigor; look for the blessings, the lessons, in each experience.

Recently, when I was starting a new career and working on my branding, my coach wanted me to create a tag line. What would best convey the essence of the message I want to deliver to others? It boiled down to three key points:

Hear Your Heart: Listen to what your very essence is telling you to do. You are happier when you are true to yourself, instead of trying to be what someone else wants you to be.

Mind Your Mind: Pay attention to your thoughts. You get to choose whether you feel happy or defeated. You get what you focus on, so consciously choose to focus on the good you want to bring into your life. It honestly works!

Love Your Life: Make a decision to pay attention to everything good in your life. The more you are grateful for what you have now, the more good comes into your life. Decide to love your life, and you will lead a life worth loving. You may not direct each event that happens, but you are the executive producer of your thoughts and reactions to each event. Determine to spend your moments in joy and do not let adverse conditions control circumstances and options for you. They can't, unless you give them permission to get you down. Personally, I don't want to relinquish that power.

I may have a new liver and kidney, but yours probably work as well as or better than mine. You most likely came into this life with pre-installed equipment that will see you through the rest of your life. That is no less a gift than my transplants. When I wake up and acknowledge my amazing good fortune to be alive and bless my new organs, I also bless and treasure my heart and lungs and muscles and bones and vision and hearing and all those parts that have been with me since my birth in 1948 and are still performing beautifully.

I fully intend to use all I have to the full extent. I am one of those old people the young whippersnappers see traveling and showing them a thing or two! My paradigm of "old" has shifted. It may be human nature to take things for granted, and I have been there, done that. Being here, doing this is so much better.

My paradigms of age, health, relationships, attitudes and so much more have shifted and added immensely to my life. I see that hanging on to old, unhelpful ideas can cause pain and disruption. My new level of awareness brings me great joy, and I am now known as the "Paradigm Shifter." My mission is to help as many people as I can shift their paradigms to bring more fulfillment and joy to their lives. Please appreciate what you already have in your life, dream big and join me in a Mission Unstoppable. Make every day a good day for you!

Elaine Ginn is an author, spiritual counsellor and professional speaker who has been an encouragement to groups of ten to hundreds for more than thirty-five years. With her wisdom earned from life's hard lessons, Elaine enthusiastically stitches together a view of the world filled with light to help people see their place in the world and lead them to a path toward joy and fulfillment.

Drawing from decades of health care experience, serving as a nurse, instructor, professor, caregiver and patient, Elaine offers her unique perspective and insights in her talks and in her book, Patchwork, *available from SeaLightPress.com. She is currently writing her second book,* The Patchwork Paradigm, *and has just launched a new podcast titled* PATCHWORKspirituality, *which can be accessed at PATCHWORKspirituality.podbean.com. Connect with Elaine at www. ElaineGinn.com.*

ANTHONY "TONY" CAHILL

CREATE AN *AND* INSTEAD OF AN *OR* LIFE

Until very recently, I was in a terrible rut. The problem was, it was comfortable. It wasn't a challenge to just continue walking the well-worn path I was stuck in. I knew it well, I had what I needed and nothing changed. But I could sense that a path branched off from where I was stuck. The problem was, I couldn't see where it was going. Who knew what was out there? What dangers, what potential failures lay in wait for me if I deviated from the path I'd been on for so long?

This has been an issue for me all my life, it seems. In many areas of my life I exhibited natural proficiency. I didn't have to work hard to impress my teachers, my parents, my employers, going the extra step meant I ostracized myself with peers. So I didn't. Why give a hundred percent when everyone seemed satisfied and happy with eighty-five?

The problem was that I wasn't satisfied. I wasn't happy holding back, so I recently embarked on a journey to understand why I do that in the first place. I've realized that it's just good, old-fashioned fear. Fear of failure and criticism, plain and simple.

After that crack about giving eighty-five percent, you may be surprised that I consider myself a perfectionist. Most people confuse perfectionism with excellence, as in: that person always produces at the highest caliber. For me, that's not it at all. If I produce at the highest caliber, I will then sabotage it, hold back, or won't even try *because I won't be perfect.*

In my experience, I have discovered that striving for *excellence* is outward-focused. It's less concerned about the ego and more concerned about being of service, about what is best for oneself and those who connect with it in the world.

Striving for *perfection* is inward-focused. It's all about the ego. In this headspace, one becomes more focused on ensuring that everything looks good, is accepted and liked. It is a need to control all situations to avoid pain or confrontation, and is far less concerned about serving.

I've always worked in the technology industry. Something I've come to understand is just how much computer networks are a reflection of ourselves and our society. The way computer network systems have always operated is a Client-Server model. That means a "Big Brain" (the server) runs everything; all of the individuals, or

I wasn't happy holding back.

computers connected to it, are called clients. The Big Brain runs the show. It sends out tasks or demands; the clients then gather up information and send it to the Big Brain for it to store and use as it sees fit. The client depends on the server to allow it to function.

So much of our lives, both personally and professionally, are set up this way, if you think about it. A set of rules is established, controlled by an entity, and we all scurry to give it what it wants. Businesses run in this manner, as well as governments, and especially ourselves. We've bought into the idea that we must appease a central control, that we must rely on it to gain approval in order to function. Maybe central control is your boss, your parents or family, or maybe it's your own mind.

It's always been done this way, so why change it? It's accepted. both personally and professionally We've been using the old paradigms, and continue to create it in new ways—the same way of working things, but with a different coat of paint on the outside.

What's interesting about where technology has been heading is that it reflects a shift in our model, seeking independent collaboration. People have discovered new ways to communicate and to learn, to develop and implement new ideas. This is reflected in a model called the Peer-to-Peer network. Instead of appeasing a giant, central system, we communicate directly with each other. We can ask our own questions, share our thoughts, creativity and receive feedback from others instead of being given tasks from "Central Control."

Because we've migrated into a mobile world, one where people have smart phones, tablets and laptops, we're learning that we no longer have to be connected to that Big Brain. We're moving away from that client-server model where we're told what to do

The Big Brain runs the show.

and how to do it, toward the model where we are now our *own* brain. We can connect to someone else directly for information without being told when or how to connect. We get to drive our own interests, seek our own knowledge and do with that what we choose. No longer do we need the condescension of a Big Brain ordering us around.

So there I stood in my rut, locked into the mindset that I had to continue down the same road, thinking the same way, processing my thoughts and wants and even my dreams in the same way, always needing approval from that Big Brain, that Being in Charge who is outside of myself. And I realized that I could do something different. *Why am I giving the power to an external beast, letting my fear of disappointing it or failing at my task stop me from asking my own questions or trying a new way of problem solving?*

And that was my problem: I'd been giving that external entity the power to control me. In my case, it was my fear of failure, of what I attempted not coming out perfectly. In computer parlance, it's was an *OR* command: *I can continue walking down this path where I'm successful, avoid frightening changes, remaining comfortable and unsatisfied,* OR *I can take a different path and encounter the unknown, possibly falling on my face or worse, but possibly getting everything I have dreamed of and being satisfied.*

I always sought an authority figure for approval instead of believing in myself, putting it out there without attachment and letting others choose. I'd been afraid of bridging the world between the black and white imposed externally and my intuitive spiritual knowledge and experience. I'd been afraid of stretching myself to an uncomfortable point, out of my comfort zone, being bare and vulnerable about myself, in order to get over my fear of criticism or rejection.

It's as if I thought that making a mistake or trying something out of the norm would result in a giant blue screen of death—all systems in my life shutting down, nothing working, complete failure. Slowly but surely, as I made myself examine my fears and why I have them, I learned that's preposterous. Life doesn't work like that. Trying something new doesn't mean total failure. It just might mean that I need more information or more experience to progress.

I choose to adopt a new model: seeking *my own* information without the safety net of an external entity in control. I can be comfortable on a path *and* have it be different from what I've done before. I can try something new *and* remain successful. I can be comfortable *and* satisfied. It just requires that first, frightening step into the unknown. It requires using the *AND* command instead of the *OR* command.

As I embark on this new venture of mine, I'm learning that by overcoming my fears and trepidations, I'm allowing my inner voice to be heard. I'm finding my true self. There is a philosophy called Principle of Correspondence; this states that your external world is a reflection of your internal world. If there was a blue screen of death in my life, it's because I put it there. I write the program, I am in control and so I can program a new outcome for myself. By changing the internal, I can create lasting change the external. It's time for a shift in our thinking.

This is creating yet a new shift in thinking and awareness allowing us to create a third model. It combines the two models of Big Brain/Client and Peer-to-Peer network to a Collaborating/ Contributor network model. In this model, a field of possibilities is created that form around a common interest, intention or project.

In this model, anyone may be the Big Brain and collaborate with many peers around an intention, idea or project for a period of time. As the intention and interest shift; new people, groups of people or systems may get involved or previous ones drop off. The Big Brain who is leading may shift depending upon the roles of those involved. A constant evolving field of possibility is created through the collaboration of who is involved, the roles each play and how they contribute at any given time.

This creates a new potential for how technology becomes a seamless tool that operates in alignment with how we really interact with each other within business, society and personally.

I choose to adopt a new model.

We are empowered to contribute our unique core gifts and talents to shared core objectives. I refer to this as: The Principle Of Digital Correspondence.

Write out your vision of what your life could be for the next six and twelve months, ideally for the next three, five and ten years. What does that look like? Where are you? What are you doing? What does it look and feel like? What does it smell, taste, sound like. Your intention is set by your imagination, so use it. Write out what you see as your purpose and your vision for yourself and your community. What are your unique core talents and gifts? Everyone has one; that is why you are here. Fine-tune this by picking out specific areas you want to focus on. For example, I listed my career, family, my spiritual self.

Now comes the hard part. Ask yourself: "To create this vision, what am I willing to do to make this real?" List what actions you can take to achieve your objective and by what date you will take them. Most importantly, share this with someone. Say it out loud. Commit yourself to this goal in a fundamental way, one you can't talk yourself out of—your friend, business partner, life coach, whomever you've chosen to declare this to will help you keep yourself on task even when you're ready to stop. When you put it in writing and declare it to someone, you're now being held accountable by yourself, because you're giving those goals and dreams power. It's easy to lie to yourself when you are in a dark room, but not when you let light in from the outside world.

I chose to focus on my career. I visualized financial sustainability, a way to create new and reoccurring streams of revenue and lead me to abundance. To achieve this I had to first take a chance on my new ideas. I had to commit to being organized and focused on giving a hundred percent to those tasks instead of the mediocre eighty-five percent I'd given up until this point. I had to let go of being afraid to try.

Now that I'm following this plan, I've started the company I've always wanted. Since beginning this process, I've had many new projects occur for me. In fact, one of them currently under development involves an innovative process of empowering the company's sales team to be independent clients with ability to make decisions, choices and contributions for themselves in accountability and integrity.

Even the business world is beginning to see that the old way of thinking with the Big Brain in charge is limiting. We're all beginning to see the value of a collaborative-contributive methodology.

By being in charge of ourselves, we're giving ourselves more independence, more room to grow, more opportunities to try new things and contribute to others. In today's world, information is the new currency. Information—everything about you, what you produce, make, share and so forth—is intellectual property. It's *of* you. It has value. It's your unique core gift and talent to share and contribute. If used properly, it can create a positive transformational impact in our world. It can help others be in service to you, help

228

companies fine-tune themselves to meet your needs, reduce the amount of needless information bombarding you.

The old paradigm of the monolithic Big Brain meant that it had all of the value; you merely existed to serve it. As we transform to the new collaborative model where everyone's contribution has value, we have an opportunity to give up our sense of control and stop trying to fit into what everyone else says we should be doing. We have an opportunity to try to reach out and allow ourselves to experience new things, to gather new information and share it in service and to invite others to contribute their unique core talents and gifts.

I still have the same fears and hesitations, but now when they come up, I feel stronger in my ability to make the right choice and not be overwhelmed and let them stop me. It's just fear. Fear is just a feeling. Recognizing and letting go of that leaves me with the simpler task of providing decisive action. It's become far more simple. Instead of letting all of the "what ifs" hold me back, locked into obsessing over questions and anxiety, now I simply have to *do*.

In letting go of my fear of criticism and rejection and realizing that what I produce isn't perfect at first, but it is a journey of excellence, I've set myself free to live life more fully. I've created my *AND* instead of being trapped in the *OR*. Now I get to live a life with the simple command: Imagine, choose, take action *AND* succeed.

Anthony "Tony" Cahill has a background in biomedical engineering from Marquette University. He has worked extensively in technology with over fifteen years' experience in medical imaging, mobile computing, supply chain, digital asset management, digital storage and archive. He received The Visionary Product Award in 2012 for development work in digital workflow system design. He is currently CEO of Cahill Technologies, LLC and THE PRODIGAL GROUP, INC and serves on many technology advisory boards. Connect with Tony at www.TonyCahill3.Wordpress.com.

KHENAN PAXTON

THE MOST IMPORTANT RELATIONSHIP

Then Jesus said to those Jews, who believed Him,
"If you abide in my word, you are my disciples indeed.
And you shall know the truth and the truth shall make you free."
John 8:31-32

We live in a challenging time. With the prevalence of technology, our one-on-one time with people is dwindling. Relationships are essential if we are to realize our dreams, walk the path of our true purpose and live a fulfilled life. And yet we cannot develop quality relationships if we don't take the time to get to know someone.

Success comes in more than one form. Material things come and go, but relationships last. Strong relationships with the right core people are worth more than money, more than fame, more than rewards or accolades. In relationship with others you learn more about who you are; you have examples and role models to help guide you; you have people to lean on in times of need; you have answers to questions; you have support for your endeavors; you have comfort in times of sadness; and you have a group of people who want to see you succeed, and take action to help you achieve your goals.

Growing up, I didn't have good relationships. My life's journey started out a little shaky. I was born prematurely and immediately placed in an incubator. My mom, who had given birth to my three siblings before conceiving me, went to court a few days after my birth and spent the first three months of my life in jail.

My childhood home was dysfunctional at best and terrifying at worst. I still recall in vivid detail the day my father whipped me with a belt buckle so severely I was hospitalized. I was just five years old. Mom had him arrested for child abuse and he

Growing up, I didn't have good relationships.

was sent to prison for a few years. When he was released from prison, he moved back in with us and the fighting started. Mom's way of protecting us was to keep moving—but no matter where we moved, my father would always find us and move back in.

At times, my siblings and I were very fearful of our father. The beatings continued, and every time Mom intervened, he would beat her too. She developed a real fear of my father hurting us, and in this desperate state contacted a social worker to place all six of her children in foster care. By making this difficult decision, she hoped to save us.

After entering the foster care system, my relationships remained challenged and, at times, volatile. I had a hard time adjusting to my new life and, because of this, I was beaten by a foster care employee. I remember standing in line with the other children and receiving a slap so hard my head hit the wall. This was a very emotional time for me. I was confused, damaged and suffering from the shock of it all.

Finally, when I was eight years old, this chapter of my life ended with the passing of my father. My mom was able to get all of her children out of foster care and bring us back together as a family. During this traumatic experience, I developed coping mechanisms. My parents' fights had caused me to become insecure. As I transitioned from puberty to adolescence, I felt I needed to be emotionally guarded to feel safe.

During the seventies, my mom was involved in civil rights and she was an entrepreneur. A lot of her social lifestyle rubbed off on me. I attended the Boy Scouts, hung out at the boy's club, took guitar lessons and was a leader on our local baseball team. But despite the positive changes, I was exposed to the sinfulness

I was beaten by a foster care employee.

of adult behavior. Mom held parties regularly with her friends in our home. At these very adult parties, I witnessed dysfunction in other people and realized that it wasn't just present in my family. This openly adult behavior started to affect our family, as my first three siblings all had teen pregnancies.

By the time we reached our mid-teens, one by one we were encouraged or led to move out of our home. I was caught between adolescence and adulthood and afraid of so many things. Over the next thirteen years I would struggle with most of my relationships—family, friends and professional contacts.

But I would soon meet a man who would show me the value of developing positive, quality relationships. While working as a manager at Home Depot, I met Mr. Nolan, a gentleman who became a mentor to me.

I also went through some challenges with my career; I became an entrepreneur and moved from New York to California where I gained experience in retail management, real estate sales and network marketing. While working for a major retail chain, I met a man who would show me the value of developing positive, quality relationships. During my tenure as a manager, I met Mr. Nolan, a gentleman who became a mentor to me.

Mr. Nolan believed in me. We built a good relationship, and because he trusted me, I was able to move up quite rapidly in the organization. I was only twenty-six years old and was given the opportunity to oversee millions of dollars. Before that, I knew I had the ability, but I never had the chance to prove it. Mr. Nolan's confidence in me made me believe I could really excel, that it wasn't just a pipe dream.

I was finally having some success relationally as well as professionally, However, I inside I was unfulfilled. I tried the usual adult things like hanging out on the weekends with friends or indulging myself with the things that I enjoyed, but I was still not settled inside.

Then one day, I was asked to attend a church service with a co-worker and friend. Not knowing what to expect, I was skeptical, but I agreed. While I attended the church service, something happened within me. It seemed as if I belonged there, and I thought, "This is what family is all about."

I didn't fully comprehend what I was experiencing until I moved back to New York where I met a pastor named Dr. Youngblood, and started to attend church weekly. On Tuesday nights they spoke about issues for men, and there I met men

I felt a desire to serve in a whole new way.

who had lived through similar experiences, men who had the same challenges and questions I had. Developing a network of spiritually-minded men I could relate to was a key factor in my healing, but my relationship with Dr. Youngblood was truly life-changing. He became a father figure to me, and his mentorship helped shape my dreams.

I received Christ in life and dedicated my children to Him. This would be the beginning of a spiritual battle inside of me. I felt a desire to serve in a whole new way and was starting to understand why I had conflicting relationships most of my adult life. I had an insatiable desire to help others; somehow this caused of some of the greatest misunderstandings with the people I love. I learned that what I believed to be love while growing up was *not* love. And, because of the confusion associated with those years, I had developed the need to be in control. With the help of my church community and Dr. Youngblood, I was able to face all of this and heal my past.

Learning who Jesus Christ was established what I wanted. With biblical principles governing my life, I realized there was more to relationships than just blood and connections with friends. There was my relationship with Christ—the most

**God wants us to have a
relationship with him.**

important relationship. With Dr. Youngblood guiding me and Christ in my heart, I began a mission to understand the needs of others and to help them rise up from their circumstances. I became a servant.

As I nurtured and strengthened my relationship with God by reading scriptures regularly, praying, worshiping and fellowship, it became real. God revealed truths to me, truths about relationships and why we struggle. By not getting caught up in religion, but by putting in the time to understand who He was, I was able to focus on the relationships He wants us to have.

Through my relationship with God, I was able to see that, though my father was abusive, he also cared for us. He was prideful and wanted to be respected, but he always provided for us. I was able to make peace with my father and with the past.

Throughout my thirties, I was driven to accomplish great things. I managed a multi-million dollar retail chain, became a successful mortgage broker and managed the development of numerous real estate projects. Over the years, I grew stronger in spirit and in 2001, I was led to start Sovereign Ministries, Inc., a faith-based Christian organization dedicated to working with young people. I began homeschooling my seven children in order to teach them biblical truths. My wife and I became active in church planning, youth mentoring and coaching.

Today, when I mentor youth, I focus on three core areas: spirituality, health and education, in that order. Without spirituality, everything is a struggle. God wants us to have a relationship with Him. Since He is the author of all things, then He is best to teach us how to have these relationships. The more we work on having a relationship with the Father in heaven, the more we understand people.

Giving is the main step toward building solid relationships. If you're giving to someone, you're building yourself. That's what helped me—I gave more. I gave to my family, to friends. Not just material things—I gave my time, my energy and my love. I believe we should value life and the relationships we have with others, that we should pour the goodness of our lives into them.

Now just imagine having genuine, loving relationships with the people you love, with clients, with colleagues, with role models. How different would your life be? How much easier and faster could you reach your goals? How much more peaceful would your life be?

Relationships are priceless and a key component of any great success story. And your most important relationship is with God. From Him, you will learn how to be in relationship with others, even those people who have hurt you in the past, even those people who seem out of reach. As all things, it begins with Him.

Khenan Paxton is the executive director and founder of the Kingdom Mentoring Center, Inc. As a mentor, spiritual counselor and inspirational coach, he has dedicated his life to working with at-risk young men and women. He is creative and innovative and is a vibrant force in mentoring our young people. Over the past fifteen years, he has developed the core principles of effective mentoring, spirituality, health and education.

A well-known mentoring advocate, Khenan has published a blog for the past ten years and speaks frequently on topics such as: how to build solid relationships; have you received your spiritual awakening; how optimism and determination lead to a rewarding life; and how being passionate can make you very extraordinary. About his mentoring mission, Khenan states: "There's never been more of a need for effective and inspiring leadership than there is now. I'm excited about mentoring to our young minds, and I want to encourage you to become part of this great opportunity. I am thankful for the privilege to make a big impact in the lives of those we serve."

Since founding Kingdom Mentoring, Inc. in 2001, Khenan has worked extensively with various community organizations in the metropolitan Atlanta area, developing outreach programs while serving as fiscal manager. Before dedicating his life to mentoring, Khenan spent twenty-five years working as a tax accountant. He is currently a freelance chief financial officer, offering his services through the family's firm the Paxton Financial Corporation.

Khenan Paxton is currently planning the 2015 release of his new book and collaboration: A Healing for the Brotherhood. Connect with Kingdom Mentoring, Inc. at www.KingdomMentoring.org.

JACKIE E. MAYFIELD

ANGELS MAKE OUR PATH

"Get under the bed, quick! The night riders are coming." This was my introduction to Selma, Alabama in 1955. I was seven years old, and I'll never forget that night. Emmett Till had been murdered not far away. Jim Clark had just started his infamous ten-year reign as the sheriff of Selma. Martin Luther King, Jr., Rosa Parks, E.D. Nixon and the Blacks in Montgomery were sick and tired of being sick and tired. I didn't know any of this.

I was in Selma with my Grandmother Bey-Bey to get my father, Silas Anderson, out of jail. He'd been accused of "being with a white woman." The white woman my father had "been with" was his wife, my mother, Bey-Bey's daughter Louella. Bey-Bey was summoned to prove that my mother wasn't white, just light skinned. Now, we were ducking under beds for fear of the night riders and praying that my father would be released from jail.

Bey-Bey prevailed. My father Silas was released. Then she gave Louella and Silas a bit of advice. "Y'all need to leave this-here place."

I was leaving with Bey-Bey. I was the apple of her eye, and in her mind she saw a special place for me. Little did I know that special place would be shared with all of my brothers and sisters when, four years after Selma, my mother died, and Bey-Bey and Grandpa

Louis took us all in. Now, we really were Bey-Bey 's kids—all nine of us.

Grandpa Louis was one of the many angels who, over the course of my life, would come to my aid in times of trouble. He helped to define and defend me, the boy and the man. He was a stonemason finisher and could build anything. Early every morning, Grandpa Louis would leave home rolling his wheelbarrow to the rhythmic sound of his tools bumping the edges. Late every evening, he'd return with money to keep the family afloat. I didn't know at the

**We were ducking under beds
for fear of the night riders.**

time that this was my first and daily lesson in business. He had no boss; he punched no clock. He left with his skill and his will. Service rendered; he returned with money to make our meager dreams come true. He didn't seem afraid; he didn't complain, and some of the stone walls he built are still standing in Bogalusa today. Even more are still standing in me.

I came of age as a teenager in that crowded shotgun house in Bogalusa, Louisiana—the place that the *Nation* magazine called Klan Town.

On February 21, 1964, three men set out from Jonesboro traveling three hundred miles southeast to Bogalusa. There were no superhighways—just two-lane backwoods highways through small towns and known Klan strongholds—like Abbeville, Ville Platte and Turkey Creek. Frederick Douglas Kirkpatrick, Ernest (Chilly Willy) Thomas, and Congress of Racial Equity (CORE) worker Charles Fenton had been key in creating a local armed self-defense league to protect those in the Jonesboro Civic and Voters League, as well as other Black citizens, from police and Klan violence. They called their group the Deacons for Defense and Justice.

Waiting for their safe arrival was a huge crowd at the Union Hall. Chief among them were organizers and activists from the old NAACP, the Bogalusa Civic and Voter's League (BCVL) and CORE as well as youth who often defied their parents' warnings to stay home and not get involved.

A.Z. Young, Robert Hicks and Charlie Sims were on hand to greet the three Deacons from Jonesboro. Kirkpatrick took the podium. He placed a Bible on one side of the podium and a gun on the other as he stressed, "We have to defend our children."

"Yes," the crowd roared back. The roar seemed muffled as I drifted back to the night riders in Selma and, most of all, to the blood in the basement.

Momma had a miscarriage in Lufkin, Texas in 1957. Bey-Bey grabbed me and my sister Gloria and jumped on the first bus to Lufkin. After we arrived, Momma took a turn for the worst. When they rushed her to the hospital, the white nurses and doctors refused to see her in the main facility; instead they shunted her to the basement where the "Negras" were seen.

By the time they transferred her to the ill-equipped "Negra" section, it was too late. This form of murder-by-neglect was all too common. Thousands of Black men and women died because white-controlled hospitals refused to care for Blacks properly, if at all.

The images of Momma's blood running in the basement connected me deeply to what the Jonesboro Deacons were saying and became a metaphor for white injustice and brutality. A few months after this meeting with the Jonesboro Deacons in '64,

My angels stepped up to the challenge.

though I was a straight A student, I dropped out of school partly to help support my family, and mostly to get involved with the movement in a vigorous way to avenge the blood in the basement.

However, this was Klan-Town. Over the months and into the summer, the Klan under various uniforms and badges, including the FBI's, was successful in killing and intimidating many Black and white civil rights workers.

Again and again the armed Deacons stood up to the Klan. In the end the Deacons for Defense and Justice made their memory a legacy, and they made a real man of me. They showed me what love of self and family and community really is. They showed me that family is not just your nuclear family, and that commitment and devotion are more than prayers and nice-sounding words. They showed me the power of love for justice—a justice for which they lived and for which they were willing to die.

This commitment to family and community, this love for justice, was to become the foundation upon which I would build my businesses and is the chief reason that I've been successful. In business, you have to believe in something bigger than you. You have to build a business that really serves others, and sometimes you have to fight to keep your business standing against the inimical forces that seek to kill it.

After Bey-Bey died, Grandpa Louis told me that my father Silas would take me and my brothers and sisters to live with him and his new wife Gloria in Newton, Texas.

"What? Leaving Bogalusa? The movement? Grandpa Louis?" I did not want to leave.

To persuade me, he and Aunt Vee told me I was needed to help protect the others. We helped load our "just-have-to-have" belongings on to Daddy's stump-hauling truck. Going down Highway 190, we must have looked like the Beverly Hillbillies.

Friends had told me of a new Manpower Project jobs training program. If I was selected, they would teach me automatic transmission repair and pay me forty dollars per week to attend. I wasn't interested in automatic transmissions, but I needed the money. Though I'd never driven a car, I took to transmission repair like Michael Jackson to a stage. The movement had broadened me, aged me, almost killed me and, at the same time, given me a life and maturity beyond my years.

During this time, I met a young woman with the complexion of my Sudanese-looking grandmother. Exceedingly beautiful, her name was Bessie.

One day I got a call from Bessie. She said, "Jackie, I'm pregnant, and I just want to know what you're going to do?" "Of course," I said. "I'm gonna do the right thing." The right thing was marriage, which was the farthest thing from my mind at the time. Some of my family didn't want me to marry her, but I did genuinely like her, and I knew what it was like to grow up without my father. That wasn't going to happen to my child! Bessie and I would be married. But how would I take care of my family?

Start walking in the direction of your goals, and God will send angels.

I couldn't get a job. No one would hire me. If they did, once they learned about my activist past, I'd be escorted to the door. This happened time and time again. I'd have to create a job. But with no money and in a hostile, racist, mostly rural environment, the deck was stacked against me.

My angels stepped up to the challenge. I was introduced to the educator, Robert Miles. "Jackie, I heard that you fix automatic transmissions," he said.

"Yes I can," I responded.

Understandably, Mr. Miles looked at me with a jaundiced eye. Few mechanics were skilled in automatic transmission repair; fewer still were nineteen years old. "Tell you what," he said, "I got an Oldsmobile with a broken Slim-Jim transmission. I am going to let you show me what you can do. Go ahead and fix it."

Grateful for the opportunity to prove myself, I said, "Thank you for your confidence in me, I will not let you down."

And I didn't. Through Mr. Miles, I met Mr. Floyd. When I told Mr. Floyd I was looking for a job, he introduced to Mr. John T. Nelson, who offered me a position working sixty-forty fixing transmissions at his gas station in Orange, Texas. When Mr. Nelson passed away, I had an opportunity to take over ownership, but did not have the means to do so. Mr. Rhodes, who had been observing me for a year or two, took interest and provided the necessary investment I needed for inventory and gas in order to open. From Bogalusa to Newton to Orange, starting first as an automatic transmission specialist, then as owner of a Phillips 66 service station and garage at only twenty-one years of age. I kept moving and created the largest Black insurance sales force for United Companies out of Baton Rouge. Obstacles became steppin' stones.

Every year I'd have an appreciation celebration for my insurance sales team. One particular celebration stands out. It had been an especially good year; the place was packed. I'd finished what I thought was a great motivational speech when my youngest sister, Jenna, took the floor and expressed how proud she was of me, and my accomplishments. Watching and listening to Jenna, suddenly I saw a vision of my mother, Louella, come over her. As beautiful as ever, she too was beaming with the pride.

She said, "I'm proud of you," and then, "I love you," and I became weak in the knees.

Later, as I reflected on the day, I realized that somewhere between the "I'm proud of you" and "I love you," my mother slipped in another message: "Jackie, remember that you didn't get to this pinnacle alone!"

I had always been grateful for the opportunities, help and advice given to me. But after my mother's admonition, I could more clearly see the angels that God had placed in my path to help me rise to success. Her message has become my constant refrain, and those who know me have heard it many times:

"All you got to do is pick up your bed and walk. You don't have to know all of how you will get there; just start. Start walking in the direction of your goals, and God will send angels to help you get there. No, I'm not talking just about heavenly angels; there will be people. You may not recognize them at first, but they'll be just what's needed to move you forward along your path to success."

No matter how difficult the road; no matter how strong and numerous the opposition; no matter how dangerous the territory; no matter how limited your circumstances, you too have angels that will help you rise up and claim the successful life you were born to live. Have you seen them? Have you taken their hand up, their gift, their protection and their wisdom and used it to get further on down your path? Have you thanked them? Have you lived up to their belief in your abilities to succeed?

Recognize your angels. Listen to them. Appreciate them. You did not get to where you are alone. Let that truth not just be a comfort to you, let it light a fire under you; let it move you to reach the highest of heights!

One of the foremost advocates of business ownership, Jackie E. Mayfield was born in Bogalusa, Louisiana in 1948. A child of the civil rights movement, he made a lifetime commitment to self-empowerment for people and is today nationally-known as the "entrepreneur's bookkeeper and income tax preparer." He is also nationally known as an empowerment specialist. Using his proven "Business Start-to-Success" method, Jackie has coached and helped more than four hundred aspiring and established entrepreneurs achieve greater levels of success in the business world.

In 1982, he started ComproTax (www.ComproTax.net), which became the nation's largest Black-owned income tax preparation and bookkeeping service. ComproTax is a multi-million dollar business with more than 220 franchise offices nationwide. He combines superior knowledge of the tax-code, bookkeeping procedures and the ways of business to make sure entrepreneurs are financially sound and protected.

The Breakthrough Bible College in Washington, D.C. honored Jackie with its highest and most prestigious award, the Doctorate of Humane Letters for his efforts to improve the economic condition of African Americans. A prolific speaker, teacher and trainer, he has written several DVDs and CDs, including The Spiritual Aspects of Selling. He is the principal producer/director of The 21st Century Underground Railroad: Digital Video Magazine. His book series Blood in the Basement: From Paralyzing Hate to Prosperity is available at www.BloodInTheBasement.com. Connect with Jackie at www.MayfieldETG.com.